WELCOME

"Old age ain't no place for sissies" – Bette Davis

The older folks in our lives can teach us a lot about how we should live. Slow down a little. Take a nap. Eat seconds of dessert. Feed a pigeon. They've done years of learning for us, and if we listen, we'll discover much more than the recipe for grandma's fruitcake.

This issue of *Kinfolk*—the Aged Issue—contains rituals of the past and musings on the future. One writer laments that inevitable day you realize you're turning into your mother, while another reflects on the way life—like fruit—is about picking that perfectly ripe moment. We suggest ways to feel older instead of younger and let you gaze into the history-filled eyes of people who have lived a full century. Our favorite chefs share family recipes they've perfected over time, we reinvent wintertime dishes our grandmothers used to (often badly) make and create a menu designed for eating with and without dentures. There are gray hairs and salt-and-pepper beards, napping tips and ancient culinary tools. The connection? Everything in this issue gets better, or tastier, with age.

Growing older doesn't just mean adding candles to our birthday cakes. Wrinkles tell stories, as do the grooves in our cutting boards and the photographs in our albums. As these experiences amass, filling our minds with tales to one day tell our own children, they make us grow inch by glacial inch. While many magazines pressure us to hang on to youth, we believe we're made fuller by the people, meals and traditions of things past.

Other aspects of life also improve with a little time: wine, truffles, a good jar of sauerkraut. Simplicity in design survives longer than the complex. Processes such as fermenting, pickling and curing bring out the flavors in foods through extending their lives. Trees grow taller and wider as grandfathers stoop, and yet there's a mature beauty in all of these objects and people.

While making this issue, we've gleaned kindhearted advice from the elderly friends in our lives, and they all speak the same message: Love a lot, laugh often and once you're over the peak of that hill, prepare for life to pick up pace as gravity brings you rolling back down the other side. So please: Pour yourself a hot drink, curl up on the couch and enjoy our fresh take on old things.

NATHAN WILLIAMS & GEORGIA FRANCES KING

NATHAN WILLIAMS
Editor in Chief & Creative Director
Portland, Oregon

GEORGIA FRANCES KING
Editor
Portland, Oregon

AMANDA JANE JONES
Lead Designer
Chicago, Illinois

GAIL O'HARA
Managing Editor
Portland, Oregon

JENNIFER JAMES WRIGHT
Art Director
Portland, Oregon

DOUG BISCHOFF
Business Operations
Portland, Oregon

KATIE SEARLE-WILLIAMS
Business Manager
Portland, Oregon

JOANNA HAN
Deputy Editor
Portland, Oregon

PAIGE BISCHOFF
Accounts Payable & Receivable
Portland, Oregon

JULIE POINTER
Community Director
Portland, Oregon

ASIA RIKARD
Service Manager
Portland, Oregon

ANDREW GALLO
Filmmaker
Portland, Oregon

CARISSA GALLO
Photographer
Portland, Oregon

MARÍA DEL MAR SACASA
Recipe Editor
New York, New York

SAKIKO SETAKA
Kinfolk Japan Assistant
Tokyo, Japan

HANNA PETTERSEN
Editorial Assistant
Portland, Oregon

JORDAN HERNANDEZ
Editorial Assistant
Portland, Oregon

KATIE STRATTON
Painter
Dayton, Ohio

ROMY ASH
Writer
Melbourne, Australia

NEIL BEDFORD
Photographer
London, United Kingdom

RYAN BENYI
Photographer
Queens, New York

LUISA BRIMBLE
Photographer
Sydney, Australia

SARAH BURWASH
Illustrator
Nova Scotia, Canada

WAI HON CHU
Writer
New York, New York

BRITT CHUDLEIGH
Photographer
Salt Lake City, Utah

JUSTIN CHUNG
Photographer
New York, New York

LIZ CLAYTON
Writer
Brooklyn, New York

KATRIN COETZER
Illustrator
Cape Town, South Africa

DAVID COGGINS
Writer
New York, New York

JULIE MARIE CRAIG
Photographer
St. Helena, California

CARLY DIAZ
Writer
Portland, Oregon

TRAVIS ELBOROUGH
Writer
London, United Kingdom

PARKER FITZGERALD
Photographer
Portland, Oregon

ROSE FORDE
Stylist
London, United Kingdom

ALICE GAO
Photographer
New York, New York

JIM GOLDEN
Photographer
Portland, Oregon

MICHAEL GRAYDON
Photographer
Toronto, Canada

NIKOLE HERRIOTT
Photographer
Toronto, Canada

INDIA HOBSON
Photographer
London, United Kingdom

KIRSTIN JACKSON
Writer
Oakland, California

KATE S. JORDAN
Prop Stylist
Pound Ridge, New York

MOLLIE KATZEN
Writer
Berkeley, California

VISHAL MARAPON
Photographer
Vancouver, Canada

RILEY MESSINA
Florist & Stylist
Portland, Oregon

TARA O'BRADY
Writer
St. Catharines, Canada

YOTAM OTTOLENGHI
Writer
London, United Kingdom

REBECCA PARKER PAYNE
Writer
Richmond, Virginia

NIKAELA MARIE PETERS
Writer
Winnipeg, Canada

DANIEL SEARING
Writer
Washington, D.C.

KELSEY B. SNELL
Proofreader
Washington, D.C.

SHANTANU STARICK
Photographer
Brisbane, Australia

KARSTEN THORMAEHLEN
Photographer
Wiesbaden, Germany

ALICE WATERS
Writer
Berkeley, California

DIANA YEN
Writer & Food Stylist
New York, New York

ONE

1
WELCOME

2
KINFOLK COMMUNITY

8
HANDS OF TIME: A PHOTO ESSAY THAT TELLS
STORIES THROUGH CENTENARIANS' FINGERS
Karsten Thormaehlen

12
SLOW GROWTH: AN ESSAY ABOUT
WELCOMING OLD AGE
Nikaela Marie Peters

14
AROUND THE BLOCK: AN ESSAY EXAMINING
THE TALES IN THE MARKS OF AGING
CUTTING BOARDS
Kirstin Jackson

16
SLOW FOODS: PROFILES OF FOUR PROCESSES:
FERMENTING, CURING, PICKLING AND GROWING
OUT OF THE SOIL. PLUS, EXPERT ADVICE FROM
OREGON MAKERS
Joanna Han

24
CURIOUS UTENSILS: TAKE OUR QUIZ ON
WEIRD ANCIENT GADGETS

26
RETIREMENT PASTIMES: A HANDY LIST OF
ACTIVITIES TO TRY OUT BEFORE YOU PUT
ON THAT FLEECE SWEATSUIT
Georgia Frances King

28
HAPPY AT ONE HUNDRED: A PHOTO ESSAY
AND INTERVIEW WITH A PHOTOGRAPHER WHO
DOCUMENTS THE WORLD'S OLDEST DWELLERS
Karsten Thormaehlen

34
A SOFT-SERVE MENU: A HOLIDAY FEAST
CREATED FOR PEOPLE WITH NO TEETH
María Del Mar Sacasa

36
RECIPE: ROASTED BEET SOUP

38
RECIPES: "BLUE CHRISTMAS" POTATOES
AND MASHED SWEET POTATOES

40
RECIPE: ESPRESSO RUM MOUSSE

42
EARLY GRAY: AN ESSAY ABOUT
LOOKING PREMATURELY MATURE
David Coggins

44
ICE AGE: A PHOTO ESSAY ON GLACIERS
Vishal Marapon

48
COFFEE EVOLUTION: OUR TIME LINE ILLUSTRATES
LANDMARK EVENTS IN COFFEE HISTORY
Liz Clayton

50
A GUIDE TO NAPPING: THESE TIPS WILL
PUT YOU TO SLEEP IN NO TIME
Georgia Frances King

TWO

54
THE PUBLIC HOUSE: A PRIMER ON THE
PERFECT PUB EXPERIENCE
Travis Elborough

56
TURNING INTO MY MOTHER: AN ESSAY ABOUT
THAT MOMENT WHEN YOU START SEEING YOUR
PARENTS IN THE MIRROR
Rebecca Parker Payne

58
AGE ADVICE: HOW TO LIVE LIKE AN OLD PERSON
AND FEEL YOUNGER WHILE GETTING OLDER
Gail O'Hara

60
THE GRACE OF GRAY: A PORTRAIT SERIES ON
GRAY HAIR AND EMBRACING YOUR AGE
Neil Bedford

68
THE DAYS OF OUR LIVES: REFLECTIONS FROM OUR
OLDER PALS ABOUT THE WAY THINGS WERE AND
HOW THEY'VE CHANGED

70
OLD MADE NEW: A CLASSIC GETS REINVENTED.
RECIPE: LAMB SHEPHERD'S PIE
Diana Yen

72
FOR YOU, WITH LOVE: A GUIDE TO SENDING
TASTY PARCELS IN THE MAIL
Georgia Frances King

74
OLD GOLD: A LIST OF THINGS THAT ARE OLD
BUT SHOULD NOT BE FORGOTTEN
Gail O'Hara

76
CAKES FOR THE AGES: CONFECTIONS
FOR CELEBRATING MAJOR BIRTHDAYS.
PLUS, A RECIPE FOR CLASSIC ICE CREAM CAKE
Tara O'Brady

FEW

90
TOP CHEFS: INTERVIEWS WITH CULINARY STARS
YOTAM OTTOLENGHI, MOLLIE KATZEN AND ALICE
WATERS ABOUT THEIR FOOD TRADITIONS
Gail O'Hara

94
RECIPE: PORTOBELLO MUSHROOMS WITH
PEARLED BARLEY AND PRESERVED LEMON
Yotam Ottolenghi

98
RECIPE: MAC & CHILI & CHEESE
Mollie Katzen

102
RECIPE: ALMOND MILK PANNA COTTA
Alice Waters

104
SHAKE IT UP: AN ESSAY THAT EXAMINES
WHAT THE SHAKERS LEFT BEHIND
Katie Searle-Williams

112
THE LOST ART OF READING ALOUD: AN ESSAY
ON DISCOVERING HOW TO EXPERIENCE
LITERATURE IN A NEW WAY: AS A LISTENER
Carly Diaz

114
DIM SUM DIARY: A CHEF REMEMBERS SHARING
THESE CHINESE DUMPLINGS AMONG
GENERATIONS OF FAMILY
Wai Hon Chu

116
THE SWEET SPOT: AN ESSAY EXPLORING THE
RIPENING PROCESS AND WHY WE JUST CAN'T WAIT
Romy Ash

122
HOW TO BE NEIGHBORLY: AN ESSAY FULL OF IDEAS
ON BRIGHTENING YOUR OLDER FRIEND'S DAY
Julie Pointer

124
YEAR IN, YEAR OUT: WE EXPLORE SOME
INTERNATIONAL END-OF-YEAR FAMILY RITUALS

128
HOT TODDY HISTORY: AN EDUCATED GUIDE TO
THOSE CLASSIC WINTER WARMERS
Daniel Searing

130
ACQUIRED TASTES: ONLY TIME WILL TELL.
OUR WRITER CONSIDERS WHEN TO GIVE
SOMETHING A SECOND CHANCE
David Coggins

132
YOUR MOTHER'S MOTHER: A PROFILE OF A BERLIN
SUPPER CLUB THAT SHARES DISHES STRAIGHT OUT
OF GRANDMOTHERS' MEMORIES
Georgia Frances King

134
POST NOTES: TIPS FROM THE GREAT-GREAT-
GRANDDAUGHTER OF ETIQUETTE TITAN EMILY POST

136
RECIPE: BOTTLENECKED PORK AND
SHRIMP DUMPLINGS / SHAO MAI
Wai Hon Chu & Connie Lovatt

137
RECIPES: HOT TODDIES THREE WAYS
Daniel Searing

139
CREDITS

140
KEEP IN TOUCH

ONE

ENTERTAINING FOR ONE

○

THE HANDS OF TIME

Lifetimes can be measured in all sorts of ways: years, meals, children or even the creases in our hands. This portrait series tells centuries of stories through centenarians' fingers.

PHOTOGRAPHS BY KARSTEN THORMAEHLEN

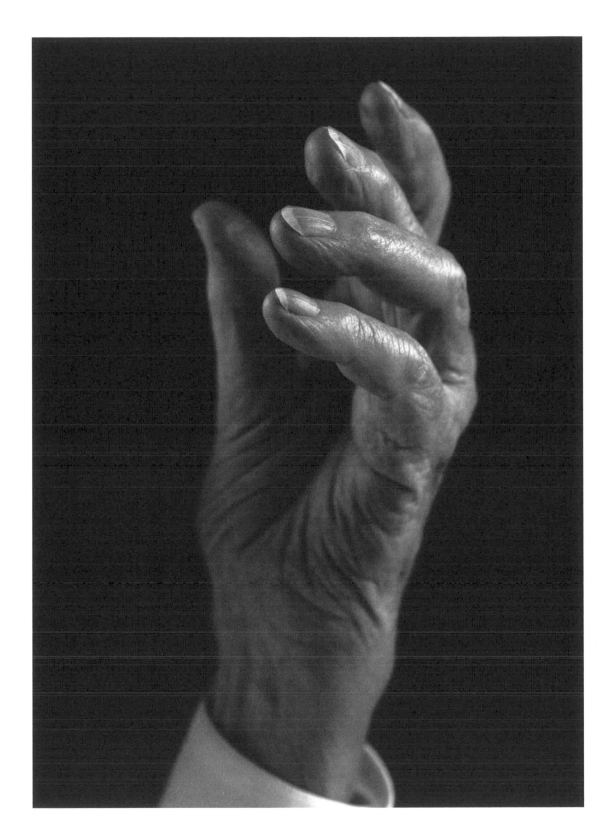

Charlotte Kunisch, 1902–2007, Berlin

Lothar Frank, 1911–, Offenbach

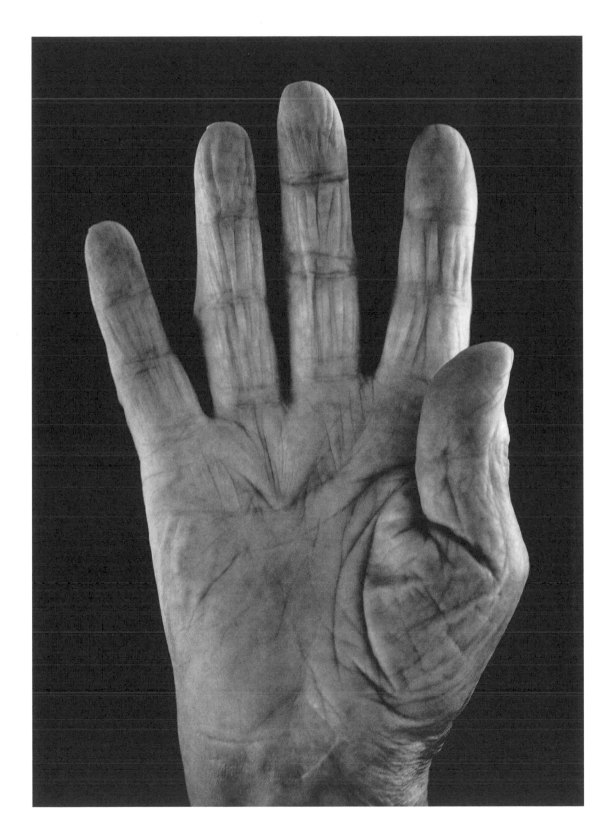

Margit Haase, 1904–2012, Berlin

SLOW GROWTH

WORDS BY NIKAELA MARIE PETERS & PHOTOGRAPH BY VISHAL MARAPON

There's no reason to fear growing old, as long as you're still growing. We reflect on the meaning of aging and what we have to look forward to in its wrinkled comfort.

I look forward to aging. I look forward to watching the people around me age. I don't mean this maliciously—I don't look forward to losing the people I love or watching them ache or slow down or get sick. I think I want to watch the people I'm close to grow old partly because I wish I knew them all as kids. I want to watch their grips on the world loosen, their souls knock around inside their all-at-once ill-fitting bodies. It seems to me that youth and old age might mirror one another in this way.

How romantic old age seems from my youthful vantage point! Of course I'm only imagining and don't actually know what it feels like. I imagine the man I love marked with age spots and skin folds that only I, in our intimacy, have traced. I imagine forgetting what he remembers and remembering what he's forgotten. I imagine being forgiven for all sorts of forgetfulness. I imagine our bodies remembering what our brains forget—the years we carried our babies on our backs, the summer we cycled across the province, the ceilings we painted, the sunburns we got, the ankles we sprained, the time we spent sitting, the time we spent laughing.

With humans it is like this: our histories recorded in wrinkles and joints and muscles and marrow. With trees, there's also an inscribed physical history in bark and grain and burls and knots that differs from tree to tree. When it comes to trees, this chronicling of time is mostly bound up in what biologists call secondary growth. Secondary growth describes the growth in the girth or diameter of a tree (as distinguished from its height, which is known as primary growth). The rings that mark a tree's age are formed by the tree's relationship with each different season. In springs and summers, the wood grows faster and is softer; in winters, it grows slower and is denser. The tree marks the year with stripes of light and dark. They record it all: The rings tell of long summers and wet winters, of early springs and cold summers. Secondary growth can swallow a fence post or hydro line, literally assuming its surroundings into itself. The seasons repeat, the climate changes, the trees take note.

We think too much about age in terms of primary growth: a linear trajectory from birth to death, graduation to retirement. We think of it in terms of increasing figures: height, weight, bank account, pension, age. Secondary growth is more subtle and impossible to measure. It's a swelling of thoughts, a slowing of limbs. And it's not only sentimental and internal. In a way, our bodies themselves measure and archive the seasons of our lives: toboggan accidents, burns from a hot stove, summer baseball bruises, each injury adding to awareness. We grow more and more alive—not less and less. And there's an impulse to collect and document and record it all. We are nostalgic creatures. But we can relax: Built into the natural world is a system that, in a way, records time and growth better than our cameras and notebooks. ○

Nikaela Marie Peters lives in Winnipeg, Canada. She is currently completing graduate studies in theology.

This elderly tree measures nearly 14 feet wide at its base and has been named the "Gnarliest Tree in Canada." It stands in Avatar Grove, a recently protected old-growth red cedar and Douglas fir forest in Port Renfrew, BC.

AROUND THE BLOCK

WORDS BY KIRSTIN JACKSON & PHOTOGRAPH BY JIM GOLDEN

Like many other great things in life, cutting boards improve over time. Here, a chef looks back on her life using different boards in different kitchens and finds meaning in the marks left behind.

The kitchens where I fell in love with cooking were traditional places full of cast iron and ceramic, cleaned with elbow grease and covered in tile and wood. There was a cabin in the Sierras with its wood-burning stove and maple kitchen island. There was a bakery where I packed tarts into white boxes and pastry chefs pounded out Linzer dough on chopping blocks. And there was my grandmother's kitchen where she taught me how to core and slice apples on the hideaway cutting board. In all of these kitchens, the slicing or dough-rolling platform of choice was a thick piece of wood.

Like the hands that worked their surface, these boards were sturdy and marked. The cutting board at my grandmother's was lightened where she often rubbed it with a lemon half to sanitize. The bakery's chopping block was scorched where bakers set hot pots. Both of the cabin's wood surfaces—a chopping block for dough and a separate board for cutting chicken for the dumplings—had thread-like scratches. These marks told stories.

After getting used to kitchens filled with natural materials, my first step as a fledgling cook into a modern restaurant kitchen felt cold. While the stainless-steel surfaces appealed to a side of me that liked all things shiny, I ached for the warmth of the kitchens I grew up in. Most of all, I missed the cutting boards.

I quickly learned that the health department went on a crusade to remove wooden cutting boards from restaurant kitchens. They were too heavy, hard to clean and harbored pathogens in their pores, according to the health department. The plastics industry agreed. Plastics were lighter and cleaner since they could be easily carried to a dishwasher and sanitized. Plus, plastic harbored fewer bacteria because it was less porous than wood.

About a decade later however, research released at other institutions found otherwise. Findings suggested that wood boards—though not dishwasher-friendly—are safe when cleaned and sanitized with hot water, soap, lemon juice, vinegar or bleach. And though porous and scarred when aged, old wooden boards actually pull pathogens away from the surface rather than harbor them on top of the cutting board the way marked and scarred plastic boards do.

Recent French research even suggests that the wooden boards that are used to age more than 300,000 tons of the country's cheeses, such as *Reblochon* and *Comté*, develop a microfilm that encourages growth of good microflora and discourages pathogens such as Listeria. With their eyes on their culinary treasures, the French continue to investigate the antibacterial qualities that people have for years attributed to wood.

I also have faith in wooden boards. At home I use one for meat and fish and several others for everything else. I've started to collect ones made by artisan woodworkers, as I know that one day the marks in my walnut and maple board will have as many stories to tell as those of my youth. ○

Kirstin Jackson has written for the Los Angeles Times *and* NPR, *and is the author of* It's Not You, It's Brie: Unwrapping America's Unique Culture of Cheese.

SLOW FOODS

Just like leftovers, many foods and drinks get better after letting them sit and do their thing. We take a look at four aging processes—fermenting, curing, pickling and growing out of the soil—and ask some Oregon experts to help us understand how they work.

WORDS BY JOANNA HAN & PHOTOGRAPHS BY PARKER FITZGERALD
STYLING BY RILEY MESSINA

CURING: SALAMI

*Paula Markus (pictured) and Eric Finley, owners of
the artisanal shop Chop Butchery & Charcuterie*

WHAT IS IT? Salami, the essential meaty element of any good charcuterie board, is air-dried sausage, cured with the help of salt, sugar and nitrate. Prosciutto, gravlax and jerky are other examples of cured meats or fish.

ORIGIN Salami was invented out of a need to keep meat for longer after hunting. Nearly every culture has its own way of curing meat—it's a primal, basic process and the best way to preserve meat without refrigeration.

PROCESS Simply put, you can make salami by covering some sausages with salt, then letting them sit for a while. They're aged anywhere from one to six months in a temperature-controlled environment, usually a cellar or basement. The salt draws the moisture out of the protein in the meat, which in turn prevents the growth of pathogens such as salmonella, E. coli, staph and Listeria. The sugar aids in the water-drawing process while balancing out the flavor of the salt and the nitrate helps preserve the longevity of the meat. The longer the salami is cured, the more complex and flavorful it becomes. "We've spent a lot of time and money experimenting over the years. Sometimes it may just take a little less sugar here or a little more salt there," says Eric. "Either way, we don't try to replicate the cured meats of the Old World—we cater to the American palate because that's who we are."

PICKLING: CUCUMBERS

David Barber, founder of Picklopolis

WHAT IS IT? By definition, a pickle is specifically a cucumber that's been preserved with salted water. But any vegetable that's been preserved in an acidic medium has been pickled, from the crunchy shredded carrots in your bánh mì to the bright pink tangy red onion on your burger.

ORIGIN The pickle was discovered 4,000 years ago in Egypt when a cucumber was accidentally left in salty brine for several weeks. Not only was this transformed cucumber surprisingly still edible, but the Egyptians found it was also delicious. Finally! They had discovered a way to preserve surplus harvests of fresh vegetables instead of watching them mold away.

PROCESS Cucumbers are covered in brine, which is spiced, salted water. The salt stops the growth of bacteria as the cucumbers begin to decompose and start to ferment. Over the course of days to weeks, the brine becomes acidic and, like kimchi, the cucumbers start to cure. The cells undergo osmosis and trade their water for saline and acid, and the longer the vegetables are kept in cool storage, the more flavorful and crisp they become. Vegetables can also be pickled using heat and vinegar to sterilize bacteria, but this doesn't offer the same probiotic benefits. A pickling tip from David: "Before beginning, trim off a small bit of the flower end of the cucumber. The enzymes in the flower inhibit crisping in the curing process, so this way you'll achieve the perfect crispness."

FERMENTING: KIMCHI

Chong and Matt Choi, the mother-and-son team behind
Choi's Kimchi Company

WHAT IS IT? Kimchi is the pungent reddy-orange fermented vegetable dish that's become less and less mysterious throughout the West in recent years. It's considered the national food of Korea and defies categorization. It's consumed at breakfast, lunch and dinner. When the first Korean astronaut went to space in 2008, he took a jar of kimchi with him. And there's even a Kimchi Field Museum in Seoul!

ORIGIN Like other aged foods, kimchi was invented out of necessity: Koreans needed a way to ensure the year's harvest wouldn't be wasted during the winter. Traditionally stored in large jars and buried underground to let ferment, many Koreans now have separate "kimchi refrigerators" with temperature control features and options for different fermenting processes.

PROCESS Kimchi-making is an inexact science. Vegetables such as cabbage, radish and cucumber are combined with salt and seasonings such as scallions, garlic, ginger, onion, chili powder and sugar, and then time and temperature do the rest. As it ages, the lactobacillus naturally present in the raw vegetables turns into lactic acid and prevents unwanted bacteria from thriving as it grows. The higher the lactic acid levels, the lower the pH content of the kimchi and the more sour and pungent a finished product you'll get. "I like to call it the 'funk factor,' " says Matt.

GROWING: TRUFFLES

Jack Czarnecki, founder of Oregon Truffle Oil, and
Charles K. Lefevre, founder of New World Truffieres

WHAT ARE THEY? Truffles are lumpy, mushroom-like forest gems with a deep, nutty fragrance. Like mushrooms, truffles are literally the fruit of a fungus, but unlike mushrooms, truffles grow and develop entirely underground.

ORIGIN Truffles exist in forested regions throughout the world, including around 1,000 species in North America alone. Most species have no culinary value, but some Oregon truffles are worth as much as $1,100 per kilogram. A few years ago at an auction in Macau, China, a single Italian white truffle sold for $330,000!

PROCESS Tempted by the musky scent, animals consume truffles and disperse their spores in the forest. White truffles require around six months to develop, mature and ripen, while black truffles complete the same process in a few weeks.

There are two main tools for truffle collecting: rakes and truffle dogs. Jack swears by the first: "I observe the forest floor for signs of digging by animals that have extracted a truffle," he says. "A hunter using a rake utilizes the olfactory senses of small animals in much the same way a truffle hunter uses a dog's nose."

Once dogs are trained, they make excellent hunters. Charles uses truffle dogs for the simplest of reasons: "Their sense of smell is thousands of times more sensitive than ours. They're just better at it than we are, and we're better at making cheese and beef jerky, so it works for all of us." ○

Joe the truffle sniffer provided by NW Truffle Dogs (nwtruffledogs.com)

Joanna Han is the Deputy Editor at Kinfolk. She lives, writes and drinks good coffee in Portland, Oregon, but is scheming to move to Sweden.

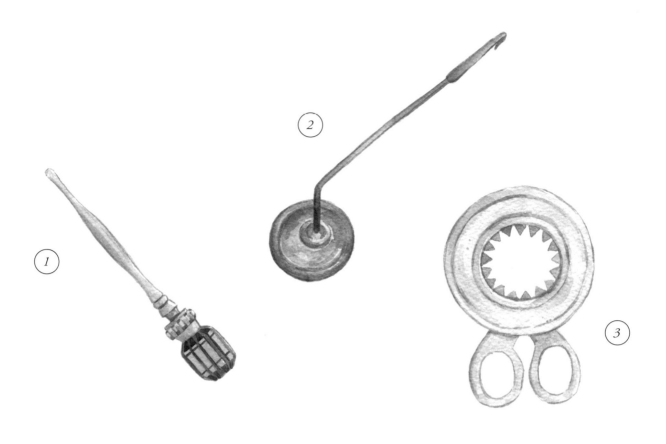

CURIOUS UTENSILS

WORDS BY GEORGIA FRANCES KING

ILLUSTRATIONS BY SARAH BURWASH

Let's play a game: medieval torture instrument or old-fashioned kitchen tool?
Have a guess at how these utensils were once used and check your answers below.

A: APPLE PEELER

Ever wanted to make your mid-afternoon snack look like a Slinky? Well, here's your perfect old-school tool. By wedging a whole apple on the end of this painful-looking contraption, you can spin the handle and perfectly peel the skin off your Granny Smith before a secondary blade cuts the flesh into flawless spirals. It brings new meaning to playing with your food, as long as you don't chop a finger off in the process.

B: CAKE BREAKER

Also known as a "cake comb," this tool may look like an Afro pick but is actually the best device you never knew you needed. When you try to slice into super-soft baked goods such as angel cakes, often the weight of the knife blade mashes its delicate texture or sends cream squishing out the sides. But this won't happen with a cake comb. Use these long thin blades to cut into the cake, add a little wiggle and you'll end up with a perfect unsquashed edge.

C: CABBAGE CORER

When the prices for certain materials skyrocketed in the post-WWI depression, it was pretty common for wives to get creative with their husbands' suddenly disused military equipment. One of those crafty ways was apparently repurposing perfectly sharp old bayonets into kitchen tools such as cabbage corers. The sides were so sharp that when bent slightly they could cut through the harder outer layers in just a few plunges. Make sauerkraut, not war.

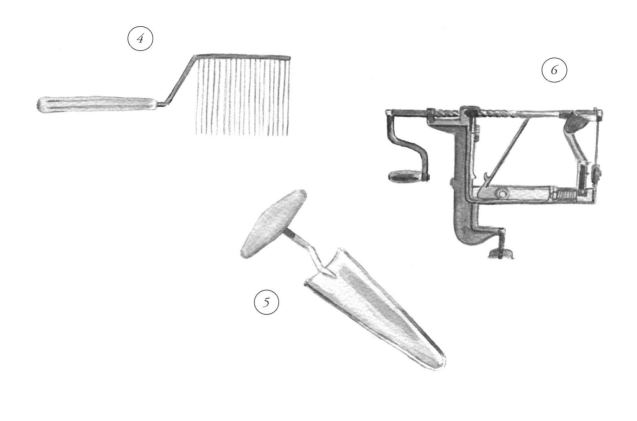

D: SALAMANDER

Before there were tiny kitchen-size blowtorches, how did people brittle their crème brûlée? Originally used in the 18th century, metal salamanders were the solution for the lack of electric sandwich presses, broilers and basically anything you now use to crisp up the top of your cheesy, bread-crumby meals. While whipping up your dinner in the cauldron, chefs would stick this long-handled tool in the coals and then use its molten heat to toast your dish.

E: EGG SNIPPER

It's an existential food crisis many have every morning: What's the best way to remove the top of a soft-boiled egg without winding up with a mouthful of shell and a table covered in yolk? The decisions! For this purpose, some clever chap invented the egg snipper: Just place the top of the egg inside the hole and "crack," off comes the top. Personally, we prefer a confident "tap-tap-WHACK" with the edge of a butter knife.

F: MOLINILLO

A rarely disputed fact: Mexican hot chocolate is superior to all other warming liquid treats. For that thick-yet-frothy consistency, you can thank the molinillo, a wooden whisk spun between the hands in a vat of chocolate, chili powder and cinnamon. The Mexicans take as much pride in their elaborately carved and decorated designs as they do in their hot beverages. The Scots also have a similar gizmo called a "spurtle" they use for their all-important porridge stirring. ○

ANSWERS: A:6, B:4, C:5, D:2, E:3, F:1

RETIREMENT PASTIMES

WORDS BY GEORGIA FRANCES KING & PHOTOGRAPH BY JIM GOLDEN

Retirees have all the time in the world for aimless fun.
Here's how to join in, no matter your age.

CARD GAMES Perhaps the reason the elderly are so good at bridge is that it takes half a lifetime to understand. If spending a few years learning a non-drinking card game isn't your cup of Devonshire tea, try simpler, slow-moving lawn sports such as croquet or shuffleboard.

UNWRAPPING SWEETS LOUDLY There is a patience for life that comes with being older. Try this Zen practice: Imagine your candy wrapper is a fall leaf you are trying to reverse-crumple so that every quarter-inch of its surface area crackles, ideally in a movie theater. Oh, the joy!

COMPLAINING As the years go by and your experiences multiply, there are so many more things to irk you: your knees, the price of milk, that FaceSpace thing or whatever it's called… Try dropping the niceness and see the world through your Pa's bifocals.

WATER AEROBICS Easy on the joints (and for the hopelessly uncoordinated), water-based exercise serves the dual purpose of indulging your urges to horse around in a pool while humoring your fantasy of becoming a mermaid–Richard Simmons hybrid.

GAMBLING What better way to squander your grandchildren's inheritance than a trip to Atlantic City? We don't really understand the thrill of this pastime, but maybe that's how you get your kicks when you've lost the ability to dance and chew.

PIGEON FEEDING Mary Poppins thought feeding the birds took a tuppence a bag, but in reality, all it takes is your stale bread crusts. Head to the pond with a bag of them, find a nice bench and prepare to earn adoration from a pack of flying rats.

WEARING MORE VELCRO …or any other easily escapable items, for that matter. The exception to this rule is a firm waistband to keep your pants high above your hips, if they're not already. For level two, try wearing some socks with your sandals. Oh wait… you're doing that too? Then add some oversize glasses and… never mind.

NAPPING Falling asleep in front of the TV can be more technical than you think. For our science-proven instructional napping tips, head to page 50.

KNITTING BABY BOOTIES FOR YOUR UNBORN CHILD As a stiffness sets into your Nan's fingers, those gloriously itchy sweaters often get replaced by scarves the length of your forearm. Give her knuckles a break and get her to teach you an impractical pattern to make yourself instead.

BINGO This is hands down our favorite elderly activity: Fun! Excitement! Numbers! Gin punch! To join in on the festivities, head to www.kinfolk.com/bingo and download our printable DIY set, then tag your Instagram snaps with #kinfolkbingo. ○

Georgia Frances King has recently relocated from her hometown of Melbourne, Australia, to drizzly Portland, Oregon. This is her first issue as the Editor of Kinfolk. She hopes you enjoy her bad puns as much as she enjoys biscuits and blackberry jam—in gluttonous abundance.

HAPPY AT ONE HUNDRED

German photographer Karsten Thormaehlen travels the globe documenting the stories behind and the faces of some of the world's oldest dwellers. We ask him a few questions about his portrait series and what he's learned from his elders.

PHOTOGRAPHS BY KARSTEN THORMAEHLEN

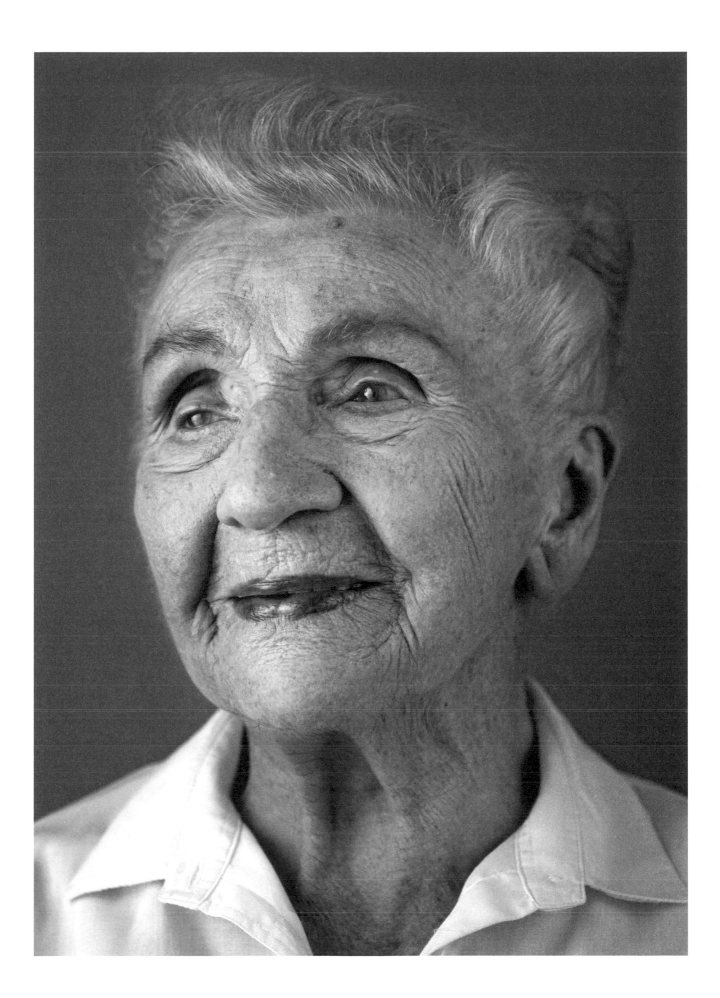

How old is old? Old enough to have a three-quarter life crisis? Old enough to remember life before TV? Old enough to live through two world wars? Karsten Thormaehlen, 48, has spent the past seven years photographing people more than twice his age—those folks are officially "old." After publishing two sold-out books profiling centenarians and orchestrating an extensive touring exhibition of their images through central Europe, Karsten recently visited Sardinia and Japan (which have some of the longest average life spans globally) to photograph their elderly inhabitants. We spoke with him about the meaning of age and gleaned the wisdom passed on to him from people born before the Titanic sank.

WHERE DID THE IDEA OF PHOTOGRAPHING CENTENARIANS COME FROM?

I'd never met a centenarian before. In 2006, I saw one in a local newspaper and thought the photograph could've been done better, so I photographed the centenarian grandmother of a former colleague. It was very interesting to take a deep look into eyes that have seen 100 years of history: almost the complete 20th century. The following year a famous hotel in Berlin celebrated its 100th birthday by inviting a hundred 100-year-old people. I found most of my models from the first series there, and now I've photographed more than 70 centenarians. There are apparently more than 17,000 centenarians currently alive in Germany.

WHAT DO YOUR SUBJECTS THINK OF WHAT YOU ARE DOING?

Originally they thought I was crazy! But in the latest series, they were all excited. They feel flattered and enjoy the attention as it makes them feel special.

WERE THEY VAIN ABOUT THEIR APPEARANCES?

They were the best models I ever had! Vanity seems to be a genetic determination of mankind though—it never goes away.

HOW DO THEY FEEL THE WORLD HAD CHANGED?

During the 20th century there were so many revolutions, wars, genocides, technical inventions and political changes like never before in human history. Compared to some recent decades, they now live the best lives they've ever lived. They are at peace with themselves and the world around them and are grateful, friendly and fun!

HOW DID THEIR ATTITUDES TOWARD AGE CHANGE ONCE THEY REACHED 100?

What can they say? They have outlived all of their friends—even their children sometimes. They have no idea why it happened to them. Although they come from completely different cultures, there are many similarities in the ways these very old people live: They live a modest life, never changed their residence and are helpful to the community. They feel needed.

DID ANY OF THEM HAVE SECRETS FOR REACHING 100 YEARS OLD?

Whiskey is a good keyword! Gin is better though. The grandmother of the head of Gordon's Gin was 109 when she recently passed—she lived to be one of the oldest women in Great Britain.

HOW HAS THE PROJECT CHANGED YOUR OWN OUTLOOK ON LIFE?

I look at things differently. There's less pressure because one has lived his life—each day is a gift and a gift should always be a pleasure.

WHAT'S THE BEST BIT OF ADVICE YOU'VE BEEN GIVEN SO FAR?

It actually wasn't a centenarian. The 75-year-old Japanese guide for my tour there gave me some good advice: "If you've reached the summit, it only goes downhill. So it is important to climb continuously!" ○

Visit jahrhundertmensch.eu or happy-at-hundred.de to learn more.

RECIPES

THE SOFT-SERVE MENU

We've created a feast that's not only delicious but also easy to chew—for those young and old who have no teeth. Don't be fooled: These soft foods are still full of flavor and will be a welcome addition to any holiday spread.

RECIPES & STYLING BY MARÍA DEL MAR SACASA
PHOTOGRAPHS BY RYAN BENYI

ROASTED BEET SOUP

E arthy beets' naturally sweet flavor is intensified during roasting. In this simple recipe, their flavor is brightened and complemented with tart pomegranate molasses (available in the international section of most supermarkets or online), lemon juice and a dollop of brash horseradish crème fraîche.

---

4 pounds red beets, peeled and cut into 1/2-inch (1.25-centimeter) pieces

1 tablespoon (15 milliliters) olive oil

2 tablespoons (30 milliliters) red wine vinegar

Salt and freshly ground black pepper

2 shallots, minced

14 cups water

1/4 cup (4 ounces/120 milliliters) pomegranate molasses

2 tablespoons (30 milliliters) lemon juice plus more to taste

1 cup (8 ounces/240 grams) crème fraîche

1/3 cup (1 ounce/30 grams) fresh grated or prepared horseradish, or to taste

---

METHOD Adjust an oven rack to the upper-middle position and preheat oven to 450°F/230°C. Arrange beets in single layer on baking sheet. Drizzle with 2 tablespoons (30 milliliters) olive oil and vinegar and season with salt and pepper. Roast until tender, about 1 hour.

Heat an additional 1 tablespoon (15 milliliters) oil in large pot over medium heat until simmering. Add the shallots and cook until softened, about 5 minutes. Add the beets and water and bring to a boil over medium-high heat, then reduce to a simmer and cook until beets are soft, about 30 minutes. Carefully transfer beets in batches to a blender along with the cooking liquid and blend until smooth (add more water if you prefer a more liquid consistency). Add the molasses and lemon juice and blend once more, then adjust seasonings.

Stir together the crème fraîche and horseradish and dollop on each serving. Soup may be served warm or chilled. ○

Serves 8 as an appetizer

"BLUE CHRISTMAS" POTATOES

Here are two recipes for mashed potatoes that use the same method with the notable exception of otherworldly, brilliant purple potatoes. Keep in mind that the more cream you add to these brightly hued starches, the more diluted the color will be.

---

4 pounds (1.8 kilograms) purple or waxy potatoes, peeled and cut into 1-inch (2.5-centimeter) pieces

Salt

2 ounces (55 grams) unsalted butter, melted

2/3 cup (5.3 ounces/155 milliliters) half-and-half (plus more to taste), warmed

2 ounces of blue cheese (a buttery, nutty Stilton works wonders)

METHOD Place potatoes and 1 tablespoon (18 grams) salt in a large pot; add enough cold water to cover. Bring to a boil over medium-high heat, then reduce to a simmer and cook until potatoes are fork-tender, 20 to 25 minutes. Drain potatoes, return to the pot on heat and allow potatoes to dry out for about 5 minutes. For the smoothest potatoes, use a ricer to process the potatoes. Stir in the butter, half-and-half and cheese, adding more to taste. Season with salt to taste.

Note: If blue cheese isn't your thing, try using goat cheese or Parmesan.

Serves 8

MASHED SWEET POTATOES

This brightly colored recipe can be sweetened with an optional splash of bourbon, making these potatoes a festive and welcome replacement for those notorious candied yams.

---

4 pounds garnet sweet potatoes, peeled and cut into 1-inch (2.5-centimeter) pieces

Salt

2 ounces (55 grams) unsalted butter, melted

2 tablespoons (30 milliliters) heavy cream

3 to 4 tablespoons (45 to 60 milliliters) sorghum or pure maple syrup

Finely grated zest of 1 orange

Splash bourbon

Pinch cayenne or Aleppo pepper

METHOD Place potatoes and 1 tablespoon (18 grams) salt in a large pot; add enough cold water to cover. Bring to a boil over medium-high heat, then reduce to a simmer and cook until potatoes are fork-tender, 20 to 25 minutes. Drain potatoes, return to the pot on heat and allow potatoes to dry out for about five minutes. Use a masher to process the potatoes until smooth, then stir in the butter, cream, syrup, zest, bourbon and pepper. Season with salt to taste. ○

Serves 8

ESPRESSO RUM MOUSSE

This recipe has a little bit of everything you search for in a dessert: caffeine, liquor and sweet, sweet chocolate. It's a variation on one of Julia Child's luxurious versions and will be a winner around any winter dinner table.

---

4 ounces (115 grams) bittersweet chocolate (chips or finely chopped)

1 ounce (30 grams) unsalted butter

2 tablespoons (30 milliliters) dark rum

4 large eggs, separated

3/4 cup (5.25 ounces/150 grams) superfine sugar

2 teaspoons instant espresso powder

Salt

1/2 cup heavy cream, chilled

METHOD Set a bowl over a pot of simmering water, making sure the bottom of the bowl doesn't touch the water. Combine the chocolate, butter and rum and stir until smooth. Remove from heat and allow to cool.

Place a second bowl on the pot and whisk the egg yolks, 1/4 cup (1.75 ounces/50 grams) of sugar and espresso powder until thick, about 2 minutes. Remove from heat and continue whisking until cool and very thick and pale, about 3 more minutes.

In a third bowl, whisk the whites and a pinch of salt by hand or with an electric mixer until beginning to foam. In a slow steady stream, while whisking (steady the bowl by wrapping a damp towel around the base if whisking by hand), add the remaining sugar. Whisk until soft peaks form.

Fold the eggs into the cooled chocolate mixture, a small amount at a time. Stir in 1/3 of the meringue, then fold in the remaining amount. In the now-empty egg white bowl, beat the cream until soft peaks form and fold into the mousse. Chill for at least 4 hours until set and cooled. Mousse may also be spooned into individual ramekins and then chilled.

Note: If you don't drink, you can leave out the rum and it's still delicious. ○

Serves 6 to 8

EARLY GRAY

WORDS BY DAVID COGGINS & PHOTOGRAPH BY JUSTIN CHUNG

What happens when your hair is seasoned with more salt than pepper?
Our writer considers becoming prematurely mature looking.

R ecently my beard began slowly, but discernibly, becoming flecked with gray hairs. Actually, flecked sounds like a light dusting of snow that may melt. It's more than that, more like a determined snowfall that isn't going away with the first sunshine. I'm in my late thirties so I didn't overreact or start strategically clipping these foreign hairs, or worse, dying the beard. In fact, I welcomed the development.

It felt like this was an easy path toward being distinguished without actually doing anything distinguished, such as chairing the Eastern Religions department at a small liberal arts college or reimagining a Bertolt Brecht play set to a Philip Glass score. I sensed my opinion on current affairs would now be delivered with gravitas. I would take long pauses between thoughts as if I were sifting the vast wisdom of my days.

I like old men: They're direct; they're good fishermen; they wear tweed coats; they take naps. Smart ones can get away with flirting with waitresses. It doesn't end there: I like gray hair on women too, from the streak (Mrs. Robinson, of course, and Frankenstein's bride) to the complete silver fox (Helen Mirren, first and foremost). People who embrace a well-lived life—the effects of age not hidden—are attractive. And fundamentally, it's just nature's way.

For a few weeks I was sailing along on a sea of tolerance, goodwill and self-satisfaction, content that I was taking the long view. Then I got over it. Day after day it became less of a novelty and merely familiar. I was slightly embarrassed that I was ever intrigued with the idea at all. For men, that level of self-awareness carries the faint air of desperation. Women have a different set of challenges. Ours is a culture that overvalues youth and combines it with fashion that moves at a relentless pace. In the middle of all this, they seem to spend a lot of time considering their eyebrows and those of their counterparts. Men rarely notice them unless something seems off, then it becomes clear that a large section of brows seems to be missing.

It's always hard to recognize change as we're living through it. You always seem to identify phases of your life after they've ended. Then you realize that you listened to the Magnetic Fields all summer, moved apart from a certain set of friends or no longer frequent that bar.

In the end, not surprisingly, I liked the idea of being old in the abstract more than the fact of it. But of course, that's not the end; it's the onset of a new reality, one that goes hand in hand with that soreness in the back, how it takes less to drink too much, the wrinkles and the rest. But when my beard becomes entirely gray, the irony will be that I'll miss the season when it was merely pepper and salt, and think wistfully how young I looked back then. ○

David Coggins is a writer and editor. His work has appeared in Esquire, Art in America *and* Interview, *among other publications. He lives in New York.*

ICE AGE

The aging process can feel slow, like you're moving at a glacial pace.
In reality though, some glaciers can shift forward dozens of meters in a day.
Just because time feels like it's at a standstill doesn't mean the world isn't
moving forward, one walking-frame waddle at a time.

PHOTOGRAPHS BY VISHAL MARAPON

These photographs were taken of the Wedge Glacier on Wedgemount Lake near Whistler, BC in Canada, which is a three-hour hike 3,800 feet straight up the side of a frosty mountain (depending on how heavy your backpack is).

Glaciers are simultaneously ancient while also being constantly reborn. Formations like these have sometimes been around for thousands of years, though the water they contain rejuvenates through a forever shifting process of melting, moving and refreezing. Their hunks of bright blue ice may seem immovable, but they're actually perpetually roaming the lands they form on top of, albeit quite slowly.

They're important to the earth too. Glaciers contain about 75 percent of the world's freshwater and cover nearly 10 percent of its land area—at least, they used to. Like the elderly people in our lives, they are (literally) shrinking year by year, so we better enjoy their beauty while they're still around. ○

Vishal Marapon grew up in Vancouver, BC, Canada, where he studied film and digital arts. He has recently developed a passion for portrait and landscape photography and also enjoys a good craft beer.

COFFEE EVOLUTION

Coffee has gone through as many changes as there are ways to order your morning cup.
Our resident coffee nerd takes us through some major caffeinated moments in history.

WORDS BY LIZ CLAYTON & ILLUSTRATIONS BY KATRIN COETZER

1889

THE PERCOLATOR ARRIVES

Frustrated by poor conditions in the Bavarian Army, Count Rumford invented the beguiling infinite-loop brewer known as the percolator, which circulates water and coffee together at high temperatures when placed over a heat source. Thought today to break most of the principles of good coffee extraction, Rumford's work still earned him a spot as Count of the Holy Roman Empire.

1929

ITALY POPULARIZES THE FRENCH PRESS

The first press-pot gained Francophone caché around 1852 when Mayer and Delforge patented a plunger pot in France, but it was really made famous by someone *Italian*. Attilio Calimani fitted a rod and screen into a pot of water and coffee, popularizing a method that would change mornings around the world. (And if you're actually in France, by the way, a French press is called a *cafetière*.)

1963

THE "ANTHORA" CUP IS CREATED

Legions of thirsty New Yorkers embraced this Greek-themed paper cup design by Sherri Cup Co. salesman Leslie Buck. Its hugely imitated blue, white and gold pattern features a drawing of a Greek amphora jug and the words "We Are Happy to Serve You," a friendly sentiment offered in capital letters as brusque as New Yorkers themselves.

1908

THE PAPER COFFEE FILTER

Using a schoolboy's blotter paper, Dresden housewife Melitta Bentz changed the course of coffee by inventing the paper coffee filter. She brewed coffee by pouring water over this filter, allowing her to get a fragrant cup without the sludge and over-extraction common in popular stove-top methods of the time.

1938

WELCOME NESCAFÉ

Swiss company Nestlé, building on the turn-of-the-century inventors that came before them, rolled out a freeze-dried version of instant coffee called Nescafé. In many coffee-producing nations, this is still the most popular way to drink coffee.

1988

ESPRESSO VIVACE PUTS SEATTLE ON THE COFFEE MAP

David Schomer opened Vivace, a Northern Italian–style coffee bar in Seattle, Washington. Focusing on meticulous preparation of espresso, this sidewalk stand changed the landscape of American coffee forever. He fully converted us into an espresso nation—all while wearing a stylish bolo tie.

2005

THE AEROPRESS IS BORN

An unlikely hit in Europe, if not on its home shores, this high-grade plastic non-electric "espresso" maker from American sporting equipment manufacturer Aerobie (maker of the flying ring toy) developed such a cult following it gained its own world championship brewing contest. Though Poland, Norway and Denmark have all laid claim to the title, it now resides for its third year with Belgium.

Liz Clayton is a writer and photographer based in Brooklyn. Her work has appeared in Serious Eats, The Globe and Mail *and* The Yo La Tengo Gazette. *She recently released* Nice Coffee Time, *a book of photographs from cafés and kitchens around the world.*

1992

THE FRAPPUCCINO!

Massachusetts coffee pioneer George Howell invented a coffee milkshake he called (and trademarked as) the Frappuccino at his chain of Coffee Connection shops in the Boston area. He'd sell the entire chain—and the blended drink—to Starbucks within two years, accelerating the specialty coffee landscape nationwide.

2013

THE FUTURE IS HERE

You can now get amazing coffee in American airports and train stations made in all the most popular fashions of the present (and past). Specialty coffee kiosks have emerged in airports from Reykjavík to New York, having reached such a level of popularity they're now sought after over chain stores. In 2014, the Starbucks in Grand Central Terminal will be replaced with a local roaster. And how do they brew filter coffee? In a pour-over cone, just like Melitta Bentz's 1908 invention. ○

A GUIDE TO NAPPING

WORDS BY GEORGIA FRANCES KING & PHOTOGRAPH BY SHANTANU STARICK

Being old is hard work. All that pigeon feeding and bridge playing really takes it out of you. Here's our guide to napping like a senior.

SLUMP DURING YOUR SLUMP There's a scientific reason why you get a little groggy after lunchtime: Your natural melatonin level (the hormone that controls your sleep cycle and makes you drowsy) spikes between noon and 4 p.m., making you prone to weariness. Combined with a post-lunch energy sap while you digest, that's when you start getting the yawns. Nap time! Just don't do any dozing four hours before you're planning to nod off for the night, as it'll disrupt your dreams.

SET A TIMER "Less is more" is a mantra also applied to napping. If you surpass the half-hour mark then you risk falling into stage 3 or 4 sleep, meaning you'll wake up more groggy and irritable than you started. Twenty minutes is the perfect restorative snooze time, or if you really need the shut-eye, go through a full 90-minute sleep cycle so you bounce to REM sleep and back.

THE NAPPACCINO Drinking coffee before attempting to nod off may seem counterintuitive but recent studies have suggested it could be the perfect power nap utility. If you drink a strong cup of joe and then take a nap immediately afterward, the caffeine will kick in after your ideal 20-minute sleepytime. This will wake you up naturally and jolt you out of a post-snooze daze.

CHOOSE YOUR NAP SPOT While couches and park benches are optimal nap territory, you can also reap the same benefits with your head on your desk or your feet on the dashboard. Or, as weird as it sounds, even a non-occupied, recently cleaned toilet cubicle can provide ten minutes of poorly lit snoozedom.

DAILY DARKNESS Although dorky eye masks are best left to long plane flights, napping in a darkened room allows you to fall asleep faster by boosting your melatonin production. To wake up more quickly afterward, do the opposite and sit in the sun for five minutes—the light will help diminish those same levels and reduce tiredness.

ESSENTIAL SUPPLIES We're not suggesting you stow an inflatable mattress, frothed milk and a binky under your desk, but keeping some napping supplies such as a small pillow, a blanket (as your temperature drops while sleeping) and earplugs can do wonders.

NAP SNACKS Before dozing, eating anything high in magnesium such as bananas or almonds will relax your muscles (bananas also contain tryptophan, which helps convert melatonin, as do dairy products). Miso soup and other foods high in amino acids also aid melatonin production and anything loaded with protein will likewise help you stay asleep.

CONVINCE YOUR BOSS Naturally, the idea of sleeping on the job may not impress most supervisors, but how can so many grandpas (and Spanish siesta-ers) have it wrong? A quick power nap has been proven to increase alertness and fine motor skills, boost creativity and can reduce the risk of heart disease by 37 percent. If your bosses aren't keen on the idea, then tell them the Ministry for Health in France has considered creating a 15-minute legal nap break to boost national productivity. *Oui.* ○

TWO

ENTERTAINING FOR TWO

∘ ∘

THE PUBLIC HOUSE

WORDS BY TRAVIS ELBOROUGH & PHOTOGRAPH BY INDIA HOBSON

Where else can a college kid nurse his happy hour pint while sitting alongside a geezer with two fingers of Scotch? Our London social culture expert has created a primer on the perfect pub, a gathering space that's endured the wear and tear of many generations.

A BRIDGE TO THE PAST Pubs have deep roots, so to enter a pub is to commune with our ancestors whose drinks were ruled by goddesses. Their existence goes way back to the Ancient Sumerians. The English word *tavern* comes from the Romans. Heaven to the Vikings was a giant pub of sorts, albeit one with a lot of shields. And the fertile Hathor, the forerunner of Aphrodite, looked after beer for the Egyptians. Someone had to—there were pyramids to be built, after all.

THE CLIENTELE Pubs are "public houses" open to all and all ages. The best pubs have an atmosphere that feels like stumbling upon a family reunion with grandpas and grandmas, opinionated dads, lithe aunts, gawky college students and a few harmless oddballs no one remembered inviting, all enjoying arguing just the same.

KEEPING IT LOCAL The earliest pubs in Northern Europe were cottage industries: simple neighborhood hovels that only sold beer or cider brewed on their premises using local stream water and malt or apples. Today's microbrew pubs have revived that fine tradition, but neighborliness is still at the heart of all the best pubs.

GAME ON Remember the days when people would gather to play cards and board games, participate in pub quizzes and exchange songs and stories over ale on winter nights beside open fires? This communal and fully participatory active entertainment tops sports on TV anytime.

SLOW DOWN Brewing is an art and fermentation takes time. Beer's origins and ingredients are closely intertwined with another labor-intensive craft—bread making—which perhaps explains why a sandwich and a pint go so well together. Think also of the aging required for both wine and cheese: Patience is needed for both. Accordingly, the greatest pubs have to feel like places where no one is in a particular hurry. Their lived-in but well-cared-for interiors, polished rickety wood tables, uneven benches and uncomfortable chairs suggest that an hour may pass here in near idleness without remorse. Just ask the characters in *Cheers*.

LAST ORDERS They may forget about everything else, but the bar staff's ability to remember your favorite tipple—colloquially known as "the usual"—is a homecoming for most pubgoers, however irregular their visits.

JUG OF ALE George Orwell took a moment out from conjuring up bleak dystopian fictions to write an article in 1946 about the perfect pub. In it, he argued that beer tasted best in flowery patterned china jugs. Honestly, why is no one doing this now?

ALL THAT GLITTERS IS BEER Even when stone-cold sober, the glitter from the mirrors, bottles and glasses sitting behind the bar in your favorite pub is enough to make your head swoon. Such sparkling lights may end up leading to another one for the road (however ill-advised). ○ ○

Travis Elborough is a freelance writer, author and cultural commentator who has written books on the social histories of Routemaster buses, vinyl LPs, the British seaside and London Bridge.

TURNING INTO MY MOTHER

WORDS BY REBECCA PARKER PAYNE & PHOTOGRAPH BY CARISSA GALLO

Whether you like it or not, you will start to notice your parents'
traits, mannerisms and eyebrows showing up in your mirror.
One daughter takes us through the ups and downs.

We like to think we are unique—and we are. In hundreds of ways, we're individuals. But maybe in a million ways, we are our parents. It didn't happen all at once for me, but the transformation has definitely been gaining momentum of late. It started with her colloquialisms, like the time "Bless her lil' heart" slipped out. It's a hiccup that rises so unexpectedly: You raise your hand to your mouth, as if to keep it from escaping. We started showing up at parties wearing matching outfits. Granted, I had always wished to be the matching mother-daughter duo, but that was in first grade when it was cool. I've recently been known to do such shocking things as praise the local grocery store's meat counter in everyday conversation and find catharsis in scrubbing the bathtub tiles. I'm helpless to this, as so many of us are, yielding without a fight to the tide of their idiosyncratic habits or sayings, wearing their clothes and looking in mirrors and seeing their faces look back at us.

There's no need to fight it, because she's going to win. Your futile efforts are no more successful than the times you willfully challenged her over eating your broccoli or proclaimed that she just "didn't understand what it was like to be a teenager." She knew what was right for you then, she knew that you would be okay and she's going to come out on top here too.

All of those qualities I knew I had of hers I began to see and accept and love. I started seeing her in the way I spent my time—with friends around long tables spilling with food and wine. I started seeing her in the posture of my heart toward others, and this deep longing I had to make people feel at home. And through it all, I started feeling like I was getting to know her in new ways.

Your mother has charted these waters before you and has learned the hard lessons. And now we are learning them, finding ourselves choosing so many of her same paths. It's partly adulthood and partly our genes taking over. There's nothing to be guilty over or embarrassed about: More likely than not, your mom was cool long before cool existed, and she deserves the credit. Soon enough, I hope to have kids of my own, and I'll wear my mother prouder than I ever have. I hope I can love them with the same tenacity and grace that she loved me.

Plus, it could be worse. You could always be like your dad. ○○

Rebecca Parker Payne is a writer from Virginia, where she bakes pies, drinks bourbon and spins old bluegrass on vinyl with her husband. She writes about all things concerning food, family, community and place.

Photograph of Bobbe Besold (mom) and Halley Roberts (daughter) taken in Portland, Oregon.

AGE ADVICE

WORDS BY GAIL O'HARA

How to live like an old person (the good parts) and how to feel younger while getting older.

HOW TO FEEL YOUNGER AS YOU'RE GETTING OLDER

HAVE A SLUMBER PARTY Bring out the flannel-lined sleeping bags, fill the room with huge platters of super-deluxe nachos and have a viewing marathon of *Mary Poppins*, *Chitty Chitty Bang Bang* and *Willy Wonka*. Why not drag out the Ouija Board too?

EMBRACE YOUR LOOKS Who needs outrageously expensive eye creams, plastic surgery and orange-colored body paint? Not us. Grooming is good, but there is nothing more attractive than someone who is comfortable in his or her own skin.

PLAY Whether you want to build elaborate castles in the sand or angels in the snow, channel your inner child and get playing. Are there any more fun ways to exercise than Hula-Hoops and hopscotch? We think not.

GET LOST Pack a backpack for the day and go exploring. Take your favorite human or your high-maintenance Shih Tzu and have an adventure. Bring along your imagination and leave your cell phone at home (if you dare).

WEAR CONVERSE When you're in college, wearing Converse can make you look like you're 12. When you're 65, they can make you look 50. If you don't believe us, just look at Steve Martin, Sonic Youth and Yo La Tengo.

DO HOMEWORK Check out a book about that subject you've always wanted to learn about (pyramids? German?). Stock up on new notebooks and pencils and give yourself weekly homework assignments that you actually want to do.

EAT GOOD STUFF We recently read about a Bolivian farmer who is apparently 123 years old and has been eating nothing but quinoa, mushrooms and cocoa leaves. Sounds good to us.

HAVE A PILLOW FIGHT We have seen these things happen in public places with mobs of grown-ups in their pajamas and we have to say it looks pretty fun.

DON'T SWEAT THE SMALL STUFF Pretty silly-sounding advice, but it really does come in handy when you start letting meaningless little nonsense get to you.

HOW TO FEEL OLDER WHILE STILL BEING YOUNGER

BE SWEET Stock your handbag with bubblegum, Werther's, Slinkys, kazoos and other ephemera to hand out to small children who seem worthy. No one will be creeped out if you have the appropriate granny-style purse.

DEVELOP PERSONAL STYLE The beauty of getting older is that peer pressure falls away and you stop giving a hoot about what anyone else thinks of you. Consult the blog *Advanced Style* to see what old-age fashion may have in store for you. This is not the time for fleece. It's a time for silver and gold. Go bold.

EAT DESSERT The beauty of getting older is that gravity will inevitably get you down and things will no longer revolve around tiny waists and big biceps. This is good news. So go ahead and indulge. You've earned it. (And if you have trouble chewing, worry not! See our Soft-Serve Menu on page 34.)

GET A FURRY COMPANION You may discover you're destined to be the Crazy Cat Lady. Or like so many dog owners, you'll become more passionate and obsessive about your rescue mutt than most people are about their children.

WALK AROUND Get out after dinner and promenade with old friends in the park. This sort of thing has been happening for generations in Italy and it appears they can also eat as much olive oil and Parmesan as they like and stay slender. Try walking with your hands folded behind your back, or grab a cane or stick to prepare for future use.

GO TO THE LIBRARY In this post-recession era, nearly everyone is on a budget. Where can you go to read free books, borrow free DVDs, access free Internet and spend a day reading 100 periodicals in an armchair? Yes, go get a library card.

DOZE OFF Put on your slippers and nod off while watching *Jeopardy*. Perhaps you're ready for a rocking chair. (See A Guide to Napping, page 50.)

DRIVE SLOWLY Slow living is what it's all about. Slow driving means you're saving gas, minimizing the chances of hitting a pedestrian, cyclist or a wandering deer and saving the planet a little. Slow driving also means you're less likely to crash into a texting teen. Grandma cannot text.

SIT ON PARK BENCHES One of the sweetest things is seeing an ancient bench with a dedication plaque in a grand old park. No need to feed the pigeons (they're gross); just take the time to sit and do nothing. It will clear your head and remind you of what's important.

DYE YOUR HAIR silver, platinum, baby blue or pink. ○○

Gail O'Hara is the Managing Editor at Kinfolk. *A former editor at* SPIN, ELLEgirl *and* Time Out New York, *she also publishes* chickfactor. *She lives in Portland, Oregon.*

THE GRACE OF GRAY

Aging is happening and you can't stop it. You can, however, change your perspective toward it and, like these silver-topped women in our portrait series, embrace it with all the energy, grace and style in the world.

PHOTOGRAPHS BY NEIL BEDFORD & STYLING BY ROSE FORDE

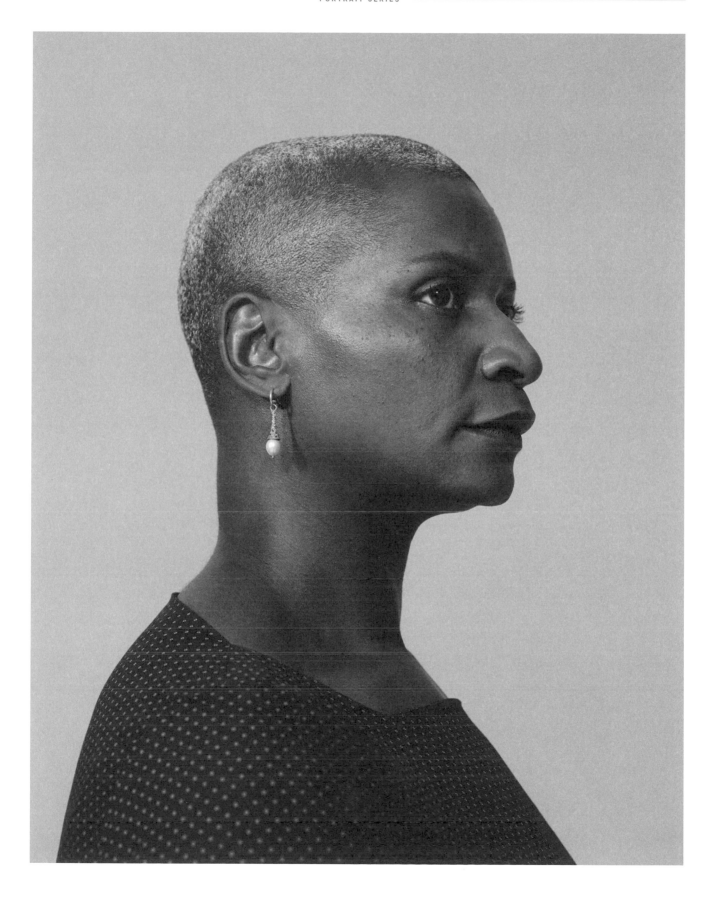

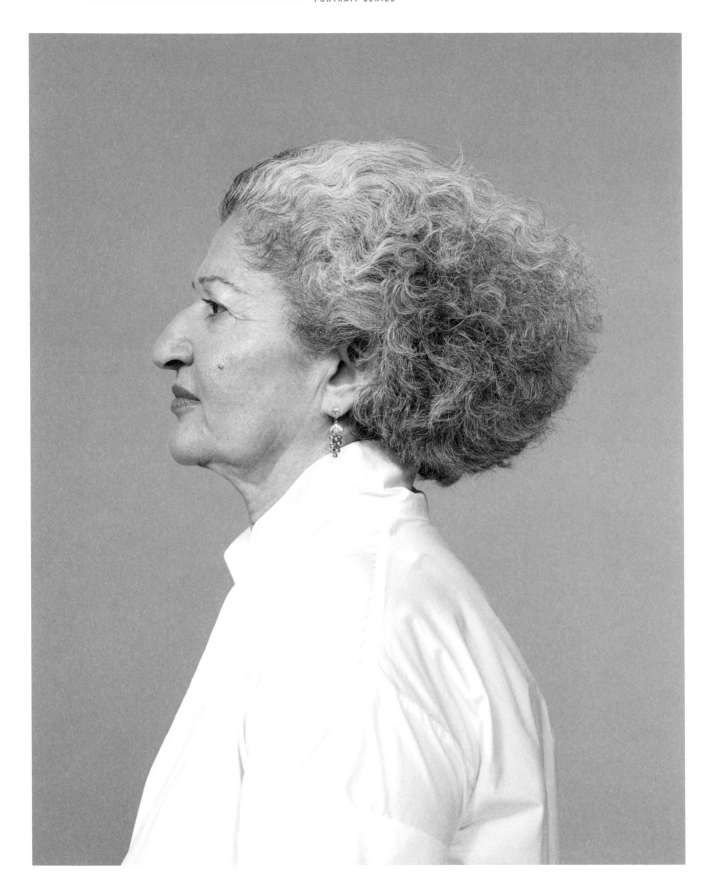

THE DAYS OF OUR LIVES
PHOTOGRAPH BY CARISSA GALLO

*Were things better back in the day? We ask some of the older crowd to weigh in
on the way things were and how they've changed.*

"I miss the quietness, the natural beauty of creation, the space, cleanliness and interaction with people and family that used to prevail. I loved Sundays where the meals were banquets. Afterward we would rest and then make a trip to the park for some recreation. We used to climb trees, pick fruits in the wild and go to the seashore to collect scraps from the fishermen, then go home and cook our spoils."

MYRTLE, 75
GREW UP IN TRINIDAD, WEST INDIES
WINE AND CHEESE SOIRÉE ENTHUSIAST

—

"People simply aren't glamorous anymore. No one is elegant."

IRMA, 95
GREW UP IN WESTMINSTER, LONDON
PINK LIPSTICK LOVER

—

"The '50s must have been the easiest time to grow up. Everything was more laid-back. There was no rushing around. Now everyone is too busy. The kids can't just play football—they need to be signed up for five sports, even if they don't like soccer."

ROBERT, 75
GREW UP IN DRACUT, MASSACHUSETTS
POPCORN WAGON CRAFTSMAN

"My mother was known for her chicken and dumplings. Growing up, my job was feeding the chickens and rolling out the dough very thin. She was of the era where you didn't write down recipes—just a little bit of this and a pinch of that. I tried to make her dumplings one time and my spoon turned green! Too much baking soda or something."

NANCY, 82
GREW UP IN JEFFERSON,
SOUTH CAROLINA
JITTERBUG QUEEN

—

"I've never, ever, ever used plastic plates, cups or utensils [like people do now]. I'm particular about how the table is set. I'd iron my tablecloth and napkins and have the best plates out. I still do."

ATHENA, AGELESS
GREW UP IN BROOKLYN, NEW YORK
EL GRECO, A.K.A. "THE GREEK"

—

"Life was much easier because the world didn't feel so big. It was about close friends and family. You felt a responsibility toward your immediate community. Globalization is a difficult concept to handle. We can't feel a sense of responsibility for the whole world. I value tradition in a world that is so complex to relate to. Traditions are important—they are something to stick to."

LISBET, 77
GREW UP ON A FARM IN HADSTEN, DENMARK
BAREFOOT WALKER

"I miss the music. They don't write songs like that anymore. It used to be based on a story, melody, harmony, rhythm and quality vocals. At the rate we're going, we'll be back to beating on a log with a stick soon. Currently I'm reliving my high school years by playing piano at a senior care center a couple of times a week. These people are my age. And I'm hearing applause again. Once you've had applause, you're never the same."

LARRY, 73
GREW UP IN GRAND HAVEN, MICHIGAN
LORD OF THE RV

—

"I've never been married. And I don't feel I've missed anything by not being in love. Of course I've had my affairs, but I've never been passionate. I don't need anyone around to tell me 'I love you.' It's never really been a great problem. I'm very independent and happy by myself, with my own thoughts and my own way of doing things. I never felt lonely or envied my married sisters—I don't think I've ever envied anybody because I don't feel sorry for myself."

INGE, 82
GREW UP ON THE ISLAND OF
FUNEN, DENMARK
BISCUIT BAKER

OLD MADE NEW: LAMB SHEPHERD'S PIE

RECIPE & FOOD STYLING BY DIANA YEN, THE JEWELS OF NEW YORK
PHOTOGRAPH BY ALICE GAO

When asked to come up with an updated classic dish that our grandmothers always made, I immediately thought of Shepherd's Pie. No matter whose house I ate at growing up, it was always the same beef stew with mashed potatoes. I decided to make an updated version with spiced lamb and sweet potatoes, cooked in a dark Guinness stout to give it some depth. To add texture, I layered sliced potatoes on top instead of the traditional mash. The finished dish is a flavorful and exciting twist on one of my childhood favorites.

3 tablespoons (45 milliliters) olive oil

1 medium onion, diced

1 medium sweet potato, peeled and cut into 3/4-inch (2-centimeter) pieces

1 medium leek, white and pale green parts only, cleaned and coarsely chopped

2 garlic cloves, minced

Coarse salt and freshly ground black pepper

2 tablespoons (1 ounce/30 grams) tomato paste

1 pound (450 grams) ground lamb

1 teaspoon ground cumin

1 teaspoon smoked Spanish paprika

1/2 teaspoon ground allspice

1 cup (8 ounces/250 milliliters) Guinness stout (or other dry stout)

2 tablespoons (18 grams) all-purpose flour

1 cup (8 ounces/240 milliliters) water

3/4 cup (3 ounces/85 grams) frozen peas

1 large russet potato, very thinly sliced

4 thyme sprigs, leaves picked

METHOD Preheat oven to 400°F/200°C. In a large skillet, heat 1 tablespoon (15 milliliters) of the olive oil over medium-high heat. Add the onion, sweet potatoes and leeks and cook, stirring often, until soft, about 5 minutes. Add garlic and cook for one minute. Season with salt and pepper and stir in tomato paste. Add lamb, cumin, paprika and allspice and cook, breaking up with a wooden spoon, until almost cooked through, three minutes. Add the stout and bring to a boil. Cook, stirring frequently, until slightly thickened, 2 to 3 minutes. Sprinkle the flour over the mixture and stir to combine. Add the water and cook until mixture thickens, about two minutes. Stir in the peas. Season to taste with salt and pepper.

Transfer the mixture to a 2-quart (two-liter) baking dish. Top with the potato slices, overlapping them. Season the potatoes with salt and pepper, scatter with thyme leaves and drizzle with the remaining two tablespoons (30 milliliters) olive oil. Bake until the potatoes are browned around the edges and tender when pierced with a knife, 40 to 45 minutes. Let cool 10 minutes before serving. ○ ○

Serves 6

FOR YOU, WITH LOVE

WORDS BY GEORGIA FRANCES KING & PHOTOGRAPH BY JIM GOLDEN

*Use our short guide to prepping some holiday goodie parcels
to be delivered via postman, not Santa.*

Some of my dearest memories of growing up in Australia involve sitting at my grandmother's flour-covered kitchen table, sipping sweet English Breakfast tea and making Anzac biscuits. Named after the Australian & New Zealand Army Corps, these morsels of rolled oats, desiccated coconut and Golden Syrup—an English honey alternative similar to treacle—were the baking mainstays that mothers and wives sent their sons and husbands during WWI. The sugar-dense recipe mixed with a lack of perishables (such as eggs, which were rationed at the time) meant they could be sent to far-flung places like Egypt and Turkey still tasting fresh out of an oven 8,000 miles away. Or if you were 12-year-old me, they were just as tasty straight from the baking tray, still warm and chewy.

Now, like back then, we normally send these bundles of edible love to troops overseas or homesick college students, sometimes packed in with a poorly knitted sweater or two. But who's to say that someone closer to home isn't just as deserving?

TIPS AND TRICKS

— The higher the sugar density, the longer your food will last, so be liberal with sweeteners.

— If you're baking high-moisture goodies, they'll spoil a lot more quickly. Try placing a piece of bread in the package to help regulate the moisture levels.

— Vacuum seal/ziplock everything to keep it as fresh as possible and separate different-smelling items (unless you want paprika-scented fudge).

— Stuff your box snugly. Shake it like you would on Christmas morning—if it rattles, repack it.

— You can legally send a lot more than you think via regular mail: As long as your goods aren't for commercial sale and contain no banned products, you should be peachy.

— However, if you're sending a package overseas or receiving one, your goodies will be subject to customs, so check ahead and always declare anything you're unsure about. Some things to avoid sending include fresh fruits and veggies (especially any citrus products, fresh or candied), seeds, plants, nuts and most meat.

HOMEMADE GOODS While receiving letters in the mail is nice enough, receiving edible yumminess clearly wins out. Dense, crisp or dry goods turn up better on the other end than brownies and angel cake because of their sturdiness and lack of moisture. And while a rosette-frosted cupcake may seem like a lovely idea, it may show up looking like a botched surgery attempt.

SPICES/TEAS For the yuletide season, try mixing up different spice concoctions to be added to your recipient's banquet: a marjoram, rosemary and oregano rub for their turkey, a cinnamon, cardamom and nutmeg blend for puddings or eggnog, or if you're feeling fancy, try making your own za'atar or pumpkin spice.

OTHER Spend a week taking snaps around town with a disposable camera and toss it in for your friend to develop, bag a tiny packet of local seeds for them to plant, or dry some leaves and flowers from your backyard. Just don't send any plant or seed material overseas—customs dogs love that stuff almost as much as kittens love catnip. ○○

OLD GOLD

WORDS BY GAIL O'HARA

Remember the good old days? No?
Well, here are a few ace things you may have missed.

SLANG Many vintage slang terms are ripe for a revival. For example, in the 1920s flappers used to call jazz bands *whangdoodles*, girl cigarette puffers were dubbed *smoke eaters* and an *umbrella* was a young man any girl could borrow for the evening. We'd happily trade in some of today's terms for some old-fashioned ones (please, take back *amazeballs*, *cray cray* and *just sayin'*).

THE ART OF THE PACKAGE Throughout history, letters were used to convey information from one family member to another, and postcards arrived from exotic locales covered in divinely designed stamps, scrawled with messages of fun and love. Time was spent assembling small gifts before lovingly packing them into a parcel—sometimes perfumed, sometimes filled with glittering confetti—to express how much someone was missed or loved. There's nothing like receiving a well-assembled package in the mail. Instead of ordering the cheapest possible item from a giant monopoly company, visit a post office before we lose them all! (For more on sending packages, see previous page.)

MUSIC VESSELS The good old days were basically a time when a handsome boy would spend hours agonizing over which songs to include on his mixtape for you, and no one would ever block your view of a concert by holding up an iPhone while taking mediocre photos of the girl bass player. Whether you're talking old gramophones, Victrolas, player pianos, mixtapes, heavy old vinyl LPs, beautifully designed teak media cabinets, album art from the jazz age or anything else, the current forms of music media out there just do not compare.

MEN IN HATS When you look at old photographs of big cities in the 1940s, every man is wearing a hat (and likely a suit and tie). These hats served a purpose: Often they protected them from weird liquids falling on their heads in the subway, among other things. As opposed to today's baseball or trucker caps, men look pretty dapper in the *chapeaux* of yesteryear.

ROMANCE Before that awful thing called "match dot com" was invented, guys and dolls met their paramours in a variety of ways: dance halls, social clubs, church halls and dinner parties. They learned to sing and play the piano and create their own entertainment. They went out on dates, wrote love letters, danced real close, got down on one knee, stayed together and didn't have the feeling of limitless options that today's singles feel they have. And no one ever broke up with anyone via text message.

BIG BLACK HEAVY TELEPHONES It was much easier to spend hours in the clawfoot bathtub drinking champagne, eating bonbons and gossiping with your girlfriends with one of these sturdy phones than a modern mobile.

ETIQUETTE The artist Stella Marrs believes that the definition of world peace is leaving the toilet stall tidy for the next person who comes along. It makes sense: Take care of your yard, your planet, your friends and family. It's what makes us human. Of course, many etiquette rules are just silly now (really, you should wear white whenever you want). Whether you believe in feminism or not, hold the door open for everyone. (For more on etiquette, see page 134.)

ANTIQUES Not only is it better to buy things secondhand (there's no off-gassing), old items are often more beautiful, sturdier and meant to last. So what if the monocle doesn't match your bad eye or the pocket watch doesn't wind? These things need a home. No need to struggle with those awful tiny Allen wrenches: Just pick up a gleaming cherrywood mini-armoire at a thriftstore instead.

TRAVEL Somehow, even after the whole Titanic fiasco, traveling on enormous cruise ships appeared to be incredibly glamorous. Even air travel was fabulous once, which is impossible to even imagine now.

REAL FILM Smartphone cameras are pretty great, but real old-fashioned film cameras produce different images altogether. Using and appreciating analog photography equipment will help keep it from becoming extinct. And there's nothing like an old movie shot on real film. ○○

CAKES FOR THE AGES

*We've created a collection of confections that celebrate milestone ages,
inspired by the culinary trends of their eras. Make a wish!*

WORDS BY TARA O'BRADY

PHOTOGRAPHS BY NIKOLE HERRIOTT & MICHAEL GRAYDON

FIRST BIRTHDAY (2012) In many ways, a first birthday party is more for the parents than the child. While games and candy may be for bigger kids, the cake is one thing that can be made expressly with the birthday girl or boy in mind. Here, simple sponge makes the cake's layers sturdy enough to be eaten by tiny hands. Since honey isn't recommended for children younger than age one, adding some of its golden sweetness to Italian buttercream makes for a particularly celebratory introduction, now that the time has come!

16TH BIRTHDAY (1997) Ubiquitous in the 1990s, a molten-centered chocolate fondant was considered the height of elegance. Here, dark chocolate ganache takes the place of the liquid filling, retaining a similar sense of richness and texture, yet sturdy enough to allow for a stacked presentation. The sponge in this cake gets dressed up in a marbled pattern of light and dark; the twisting swirls of the crumb evokes the whimsy of youth (the vanilla) against the bittersweet edge of the adult world (the chocolate).

30TH BIRTHDAY (1983) Introducing the classic 1980s-style ice cream cake: no sponge, just layers of ice cream, cookie crumble and a ribbon of fudge that never quite freezes. Whether they were made into a simple round shape, a square or a cartoon character, these chilled desserts were always adorned with swirls and garlands of something resembling frosting, and often in DayGlo colors. It was pretty perfect then and is deliciously nostalgic now, regardless of the season. *See page 86 for recipe.*

80TH BIRTHDAY (1933) Red Velvet cake has mysterious origins. During the Great Depression, home bakers often used beet juice to dye their cakes, prompting the Adams Extract Company to use the Red Velvet hue in an advertising campaign aimed at invigorating sales of its food coloring. The effort worked, increasing the market for the product and the cake's popularity, which reached its peak in the 1920s and 1930s following its addition to the menu at New York's famed Waldorf Astoria.

100TH BIRTHDAY (1913) According to pre-departure menus, on April 14, 1912, first-class passengers aboard the Titanic were served a dessert called Waldorf Pudding shortly before colliding with that ill-fated iceberg. While the recipe is long lost, it is rumored to have been a bread pudding with custard, nuts and apples, in reference to the aforementioned Waldorf Astoria's signature salad (they clearly had innovative chefs at the Waldorf). Taking that as inspiration, this grand cake takes a classic butter cake recipe published in *McCall's* in 1912 and adds ground walnuts to the batter. The layers are alternated with two fillings—pastry cream and cider buttercream—with an Italian buttercream over all.

CLASSIC ICE CREAM CAKE

RECIPE BY TARA O'BRADY

Making an ice cream cake takes consideration. A good freezer is essential, along with generous lead time, and there's a case for store-bought ice cream. Homemade certainly has its merits, but the multiple components here would require an exceptional amount of stirring, chilling and churning, and that's before we even get to the cake's assembly. What's more, store-bought ice cream is more forgiving to work with than homemade when it comes to refreezing quickly and solidly. Still, work quickly.

1 quart/1 liter (32 fluid ounces/945 milliliters) vanilla ice cream

1 recipe Snappy Chocolate (see recipe) or 1 (7-ounce/200-milliliters) bottle Magic Shell chocolate sauce

9 ounces/255 grams chocolate wafer cookies, crushed

1 quart/1 liter (32 fluid ounces/945 milliliters) of a different flavor ice cream of your choice (we used mint chocolate chip)

1 recipe Chocolate Ripple (see recipe)

1 recipe Cream Frosting (see recipe) or 1 (8-ounce/240-milliliter) container frozen whipped topping, thawed per manufacturer's instructions

METHOD The morning before serving, place a 9-inch cake ring on a parchment-lined baking sheet in the freezer for at least 2 hours. Working quickly, tear the container off the vanilla ice cream. Use a large, sturdy knife to cut the ice cream into thick but manageable slices, the broader the better. Without letting the ice cream soften, firmly pack it into the prepared metal ring in an even layer. Try not to leave air pockets. Freeze ice cream in its ring until completely hard, around 1 1/2 to 2 hours.

In a medium bowl, stir the wafer crumbs into the Snappy Chocolate topping until the crumbs are uniformly damp. Again working quickly, pull the cake ring from the freezer. Spread the soft Chocolate Ripple mixture over the vanilla ice cream, and then press the coated crumbs over the chocolate. Freeze for another hour to set.

As before, remove the second ice cream flavor from its packaging. Cut it into slices and fit these into an even layer on top of the crumb layer. Freeze the cake in its pan, covered with plastic wrap, at least overnight (or up to a few days).

The day of serving, unmold the cake by warming the metal ring with a cooking torch (a hair dryer can also be used), then slipping it up and off the cake. Refreeze the cake for 30 minutes to set the surface. Decorate the cake as desired with Cream Frosting. If piping any decorations, first coat the cake with a base layer that covers the ice cream. Let this firm up in the freezer, and then pipe. This way all the frills and swags will have better footing upon which to adhere. Use a warm knife to cut the cake.

Makes a 9-inch/23-centimeter cake (photographed cake is smaller)

THREE SWEET EXTRAS FOR YOUR CAKE

RECIPES BY TARA O'BRADY

SNAPPY CHOCOLATE

5 1/4 ounces (150 grams)
high-quality dark chocolate,
chopped

1/8 teaspoon
fine sea salt

3 1/2 ounces (100 milliliters)
refined coconut oil

METHOD Melt the chocolate, coconut oil and salt in a small saucepan over low heat, stirring often until glossy. Set aside at room temperature until needed (it should be pourable, but not at all hot when used).

Note: Using refined coconut oil means the finished topping will have less of a coconut taste, making it more accommodating in regards to flavor pairings and use. If that's not a concern, feel free to use virgin instead.

Makes about 1 cup

CHOCOLATE RIPPLE

2 1/2 ounces (70 grams) high-quality dark
chocolate, chopped

2 1/2 ounces (75 milliliters) heavy cream

1/4 teaspoon vanilla extract

1 tablespoon (15 milliliters) light corn syrup

METHOD Place the chocolate and corn syrup in a heatproof bowl. In a saucepan over medium heat, warm the cream to barely below simmering. Pour the cream over the chocolate and let stand for 5 minutes. Add the vanilla. Starting from the center, stir the cream into the chocolate until the mixture is smooth. Let stand at room temperature, stirring regularly, until thick and spreadable.

Makes enough for a 9-inch (23-centimeter) cake

CREAM FROSTING

1 1/2 cups (360 milliliters)
heavy cream

2 tablespoons (30 grams)
superfine sugar

1 teaspoon powdered gelatin

2 tablespoons (30 milliliters)
whole milk

1/2 teaspoon vanilla extract

METHOD Combine the cream, sugar and vanilla in a chilled bowl and beat to firm peaks with a large wire whisk or electric mixer. In a small saucepan, soak the gelatin in the milk. Once the milk has been absorbed, heat the gelatin over low heat until it melts. Quickly but gently, fold the gelatin into the whipped cream. Use immediately as is, or tint it with a food coloring of your choice.

Note: This recipe may be doubled for more elaborate decorating.

Makes about 3 cups

FEW

ENTERTAINING FOR A FEW

○ ○ ○

TOP CHEFS

We interview culinary masters Yotam Ottolenghi, Mollie Katzen and Alice Waters about their entertaining rituals and family food memories. Plus, they share some tradition-inspired recipes they've reinvented over time from their recent cookbooks:

MAC & CHILI & CHEESE

by Mollie Katzen

PORTOBELLO MUSHROOMS
WITH PEARLED BARLEY
AND PRESERVED LEMON

by Yotam Ottolenghi

ALMOND MILK PANNA COTTA

by Alice Waters

INTERVIEWS BY GAIL O'HARA & ILLUSTRATIONS BY KATRIN COETZER
PHOTOGRAPH BY ALICE GAO

YOTAM OTTOLENGHI

Yotam Ottolenghi owns five London restaurants and is a columnist for The Guardian. *Growing up in Jerusalem, he's mastered the art of Middle Eastern cuisine and is known for bringing those vibrant flavors to a wider audience. We chat with him about his cultural traditions.*

WHAT INTERESTING WINTER TRADITIONS DOES YOUR FAMILY PARTAKE IN THAT SURROUND THE IDEA OF EATING, THE DINNER TABLE OR OTHER FOOD-RELATED RITUALS?

We don't have specific traditions so much as a ramping up of flavors as the nights draw in. The darker everyone's wardrobes become, the colder the evenings and the thinner the commuter's smile, the more inclined I am to reach for big flavors and make abundant, generous and plentiful dishes. Barberries and feta stuffed into chicken thighs with fresh herbs and pecans, sumac-sprinkled baked eggs nestled in roasted red peppers or bursts of preserved lemon skin throughout a stew: reaching for ingredients that add a piquancy and wake-up call to winter food. Pickled walnut salsa with labneh and char-grilled squash is a riot of color and flavor alike that will offset any winter blues; stuffed squid with quinoa and dried shrimp; mixing two or three types of rice in a salad (basmati with wild or red rice) with plenty of fresh herbs: It's all enough to make anyone want to batten down the hatches and settle in. There's lots of room for bright, fresh winter salads as well, using herbs, citrus, vinegar and a few cupboard staples. Blood orange, fennel and anchovy salad is a favorite, with fresh basil, tarragon and black olives or a bright and crunchy root vegetable salad. Some of these ingredients link back to my upbringing but they all relate to the approach to food I've always had that, whatever the season, it should make people smile.

WHAT IS THE CLASSIC DISH OR DESSERT YOU REMEMBER YOUR GRANDMOTHER ALWAYS MAKING?

My grandmother's semolina gnocchi—round dumplings sprinkled with Parmesan and grilled until puffy, golden-brown and just a little crisp—is the only dish deserving of the title "the best thing I've ever eaten." She had a magic touch. The glutinous yet slightly gritty nature of the semolina, its fat and lightness, and the way it carries flavors all contribute to making gnocchi that are super-soothing and delicious.

WHAT ARE SOME OF YOUR FAVORITE FOODS THAT GET BETTER WITH TIME?

So many foods improve with time once the flavors have been allowed to come together and settle and any juices have been absorbed: cod cakes in tomato sauce; stuffed zucchini, peppers, artichokes or eggplant; braised lamb meatballs. Anything nutty, crunchy or leafy needs to be eaten straightaway—a salad rarely benefits from sitting around—but as a general rule, the longer and slower the cooking process, the longer the end result can be left before eating.

WHAT ARE SOME PICKLED AND FERMENTED FOODS YOU ENJOY EATING?

Some of my favorite ingredients are fermented: kimchi, miso paste, buttermilk and, a current obsession, kashk: It's made from fermented yogurt, milk or whey and has a deep umami flavor similar to what you'd find in a mature cheese like Parmesan. It's a fantastic way of injecting heaps of savory flavor into your cooking. I add it to soups and stews, both to thicken them and for its deep flavor. Rather like a runny feta, its tartness also provides a welcome contrast in dishes of rich roasted vegetables. It's a totally distinctive taste well worth hunting down in Middle Eastern grocers or specialist stores. If you can't get it, you can make a vague approximation by mixing sour cream or crème fraiche with grated Parmesan and possibly adding a few pulverized canned anchovies.

HOW HAS WRITING A COLUMN FOR *THE GUARDIAN* CHANGED YOUR RELATIONSHIP WITH FOOD?

It hasn't changed my relationship with food per se—I've always cooked as though it were a Saturday morning and friends were coming around for brunch—but it keeps me on my toes, thinking fresh thoughts, trying new ideas and ingredients, constantly experimenting, testing, tasting and re-testing. When the column started in 2007, ingredients available through the supermarkets were more restricted than they are today, and many spices and syrups once considered "exotic" have made it onto the shelves and into people's kitchens. It's an exciting development and gives everyone a lot more to play with in the kitchen. ○ ○ ○

Ottolenghi: The Cookbook *(Ten Speed Press)* is out now.

PORTOBELLO MUSHROOMS
WITH PEARLED BARLEY AND PRESERVED LEMON

RECIPE BY YOTAM OTTOLENGHI

PHOTOGRAPH BY ALICE GAO & FOOD STYLING BY DIANA YEN, THE JEWELS OF NEW YORK

Yotam says, "I used to go picking mushrooms in the hills of Jerusalem with my father and grandmother. We would cook them with herbs and garlic and often serve with pearled barley. This ingredient and flavor combination resonates of my childhood."

---

1 tablespoon (15 milliliters) sunflower oil

1 medium onion, finely chopped

1 clove garlic, finely chopped

3 cups (750 milliliters) vegetable or chicken stock

Heaping 1/2 cup (110 grams) pearled barley

1/4 preserved lemon, flesh removed and skin finely chopped

1 3/4 ounces (50 grams) feta cheese, crumbled

1 tablespoon chopped flat-leaf parsley

2 teaspoons thyme leaves

1 tablespoon (15 milliliters) olive oil

2 tablespoons purple basil sprouts, radish sprouts or purple basil leaves, shredded

7 tablespoons (100 grams) unsalted butter

15 sprigs thyme

6 large Portobello mushrooms

3/4 cup (180 milliliters) dry white wine

1 cup (250 milliliters) vegetable stock

2 cloves garlic, finely sliced

Coarse sea salt and freshly ground black pepper

METHOD First cook the barley. Heat the sunflower oil in a heavy-based saucepan and sauté the onion and garlic until translucent. Add the stock and bring to a boil. Stir in the barley, lower the heat, then cover and simmer for one hour, until all the liquid has been absorbed and the barley is tender.

Meanwhile, preheat the oven to 350°F/180°C. Take a large baking sheet and grease it heavily with 2/3 of the butter. Scatter the thyme sprigs over it. Stem the mushrooms and place the mushroom caps, stem side up, on top of the thyme. Pour over the wine and stock and scatter the sliced garlic over. Dot each mushroom with a couple of knobs of the remaining butter, then season with salt and pepper. Cover the pan with aluminum foil and place in the oven for 15 to 20 minutes, until the mushrooms are tender. Leave them in their cooking juices until you are ready to serve.

When the barley is done, remove the pan from the heat and stir in the preserved lemon, feta, parsley and thyme. Taste and add salt and pepper. To serve, reheat the mushrooms in the oven for a few minutes, if necessary. Place each mushroom, stem side up, on a serving plate. Scoop the barley on top and spoon some of the mushroom cooking juices over. Garnish with the basil sprouts and drizzle over the olive oil. ○○○

Serves 6 as an appetizer

This is an excerpt from Ottolenghi: The Cookbook *(Ten Speed Press).*

MOLLIE KATZEN

Mollie Katzen, one of the best-selling cookbook authors of all time, is in the James Beard Hall of Fame. After cofounding Moosewood, she's brought healthy cooking to a new level of awesomeness for the past 40 years. She explains how her childhood influenced her career.

WHAT KIND OF MEALS DO YOU REMEMBER EATING AS A CHILD THAT YOUR GRANDMOTHER OR MOTHER MADE FOR YOU?

Homemade challah, always topped with poppy seeds—to me, that's still the only kind. Mashed potatoes with gravy, decorated with peas. Breakfast for dinner on Saturday night when my parents went out and my Grandma babysat (oatmeal with raisins or pancakes with syrup). My grandmother had no concept of dessert. Wait, she did have a concept, sort of. Once when I was staying over at her house, I asked her for some dessert after dinner. She seemed perplexed, then after some consideration, she cut me a chunk of her homemade bread and spread it with a little jam. Which is a very long way of saying that my grandmother's baking specialty was bread, and it was deeply special.

WHAT ARE YOUR FAVORITE HOLIDAY MEALS, TRADITIONS AND RITUALS?

Meals: Again, homemade challah. An appetizer of sugared grapefruit halves, topped with maraschino cherries. Roast beef or roast chicken. Mashed potatoes, gravy, peas. Brownies.
Traditions: Dining room for Jewish holidays. Tablecloth, cloth napkins, the ornate silverware, candlelight. Brothers in bow ties, me in a dress. Anticipation of food that's better than usual. All of the above adding up to magic.
Rituals: Candle-lighting ceremony with incantation. Blessings over homemade bread. An appetizer after the blessings—it seemed a ritual to me. Songs in a foreign language before and after the meal, sung joyously with no one knowing what the words meant. More magic!

WHAT DO YOU DO WHEN YOU HOST SMALL GATHERINGS AT HOME?

I like to make an assortment of contrasting simple vegetarian dishes that can be served as cocktail food or combined on a plate for a light meal. My favorite part is storyboarding it in my notebook ahead of time, just because I love to sketch.

WHAT KIND OF SKILLS AND TRAITS WERE PASSED DOWN IN YOUR FAMILY?

Passion. The permission to improvise.

WHAT DO YOU KNOW NOW THAT YOU WISH YOU'D KNOWN WHEN YOU WERE 20?

1. That having fun is really important.
2. That it's important to find pleasure in every little thing.
3. It's so much better to be concerned about making others feel good than worried about whether they'll make you feel good.

HOW IS THE COOKBOOK INDUSTRY DIFFERENT TODAY THAN IT WAS WHEN YOU STARTED?

It's far more driven by media and celebrity than it is by pure scholarship, writing and the book trade. Also, it's heavily impacted by all the free recipes online. I sorely miss the days when you could discover books browsing in a bookstore.

HOW IS YOUR NEW COOKBOOK DIFFERENT FROM PREVIOUS ONES?

The food is lighter and simpler. It's also more playful and relaxed. Many of the dinner plates are groupings of smaller items, rather than one central main dish. I have a chapter of stews with matching "hats" (mini-biscuits, tiny corn cakes, dumplings) and I embed vegetables in more places than one might think possible. I've learned so much about flavor, texture and equipment. My goal was to reflect as much of that process as I could.

WHAT IS A TYPICAL DAY LIKE FOR YOU?

Before my book was completed, every day began with a swan dive—or sometimes a belly flop—into the material. Post-project, I start the day with a walk through my gardens. Then coffee and too much time at the computer. I love cooking at home more than ever.

WHAT ARE SOME IDEAL THINGS TO PICKLE?

Red onions, onions with fruit (cherries, berries), rhubarb (with or without strawberries), baby carrots (very easy, made with dill) and broccoli stems. You can pickle more things than you might realize. Pickles keep forever and are one of the easiest ways to sparkle up a meal without doing extra work in the present tense.

WHAT ARE SOME OF YOUR FAVORITE AGED FOODS?

My favorite fermented foods are yogurt, kombucha and sauerkraut. I also love some of the creative "raw food" krauts from natural foods stores.

YOU'VE BEEN AN ADVOCATE FOR SLOW, HEALTHY, PLANT-BASED FOOD FOR A LONG TIME. HOW HAS THE FOOD INDUSTRY CHANGED?

I do know that *slow, healthy* and *plant-based* are now in more people's vocabularies than I could ever have imagined 25 years ago. And that is quite thrilling! ○ ○ ○

The Heart of the Plate *(Rux Martin/Houghton Mifflin Harcourt) is out now.*

MAC & CHILI & CHEESE

RECIPE BY MOLLIE KATZEN

PHOTOGRAPH BY ALICE GAO & FOOD STYLING BY DIANA YEN, THE JEWELS OF NEW YORK

Mollie says, "Beany and slightly spicy, this recipe combines two traditional American favorites. The tawny effect from combining red kidney beans, colorful peppers and chilies and chili powder is enhanced even further if you use an orange cheddar. Not essential, but lovely."

Nonstick spray

1/2 pound (225 grams) orechiette, elbow macaroni or equivalent-size shells

2 cups (500 milliliters) milk (low-fat okay)

2 tablespoons (30 milliliters) olive oil (plus a little for the pasta)

1 onion, chopped (about 1 cup/140 grams)

1 small sweet bell pepper, diced (1 cup/4 ounces)

1 medium Anaheim or poblano chili, minced (1/2 cup/55 grams)

1 teaspoon minced or crushed garlic

1 tablespoon (7 grams) chili powder

1/2 teaspoon ground cumin

1 teaspoon (6 grams) salt

Black pepper

Cayenne or crushed red pepper

1 1/2 tablespoons (14 grams) unbleached all-purpose flour

1 1/2 cups (6 ounces/170 grams) (packed) grated sharp cheddar

6 tablespoons (.75 ounces/20 grams) grated or shredded Parmesan cheese

1 15-ounce (15-ounce/425-gram) can red kidney beans, rinsed and thoroughly drained

1 to 2 green tomatoes (any kind, unripe), in thin slices (1/4-inch)

METHOD Set the oven rack on the highest rung that will fit your baking pan, and heat the oven to 350°F/180°C. Lightly spray a 2-quart baking dish or 8-inch square pan with nonstick spray.

Put up a medium-large pot of water to boil and place a colander in the sink. When the water boils, add the pasta, keeping the heat high. Cook the pasta until *just* tender enough to bite into comfortably, then drain and transfer to a bowl. Toss with a little olive oil and set aside.

Heat the milk (ideally in a spouted measuring cup in a microwave) until it is very hot—not boiling, just steaming and too hot to touch. Set the hot milk near the stove.

Continued on page 138

ALICE WATERS

We interview Alice Waters, owner of Chez Panisse in Berkeley, spokesperson for the Slow Food movement and creator of the Edible Schoolyard, about her family memories, ideology and foodie rituals.

WHAT KIND OF MEALS DO YOU REMEMBER EATING AS A CHILD?

My mother wasn't a great cook. She was a '50s kind of cook who thought about nutrition and the household budget, but we did have a victory garden and that's where my first positive memories of food came from: those New Jersey tomatoes in summer!

WHAT ABOUT YOUR FAVORITE HOLIDAY MEALS, TRADITIONS AND RITUALS?

It's always Thanksgiving and the Fourth of July. Thanksgiving is such a wonderful moment for fall produce and my favorite time of year. I just love making burgers on the Fourth (always with grass-fed beef, of course).

WHAT DO YOU DO WHEN YOU HOST SMALL GATHERINGS AT HOME?

Something very simple and I usually use the fireplace. Perhaps I'll grill something simple and serve it with salad. I try to make it very easy and I always have my friends help out.

WHAT KIND OF RECIPES, SKILLS, TRAITS OR OBJECTS HAVE BEEN PASSED DOWN IN YOUR FAMILY?

My father was instrumental in guiding times and insisted we have comprehensive insurance, which saved us when the restaurant caught fire recently. I inherited the idea that we need to look after it because it's much more than just my restaurant—it supports so many people.

WHAT DO YOU KNOW NOW THAT YOU WISH YOU'D KNOWN WHEN YOU WERE 20?

That the planet is in trouble. If I'd known, I would have become an activist earlier.

HOW IS YOUR NEW COOKBOOK DIFFERENT FROM PREVIOUS ONES?

This one is really about the garden. I'm so proud of this book—I feel like it's the book I've always wanted to write. Now is the right time for it because so many people are growing their own food.

WHAT IS A TYPICAL DAY LIKE FOR YOU?

No day is typical. I'll often be at the restaurant and the next moment at the Edible Schoolyard. So much of my time is now taken up with meeting with people I hope can influence the future of food. My interactions with young people are particularly inspiring. I feel like this generation is the one that will make a difference and that hope keeps me motivated. I've learned that if children are involved in the growing and cooking of their food, they'll want to eat it. I've found that to be absolutely true.

CAN YOU TALK ABOUT SOME OF YOUR FAVORITE FOODS THAT IMPROVE WITH AGE?

Well, so many of the fermented products: cheese, salumi, wine, of course. But I also love pickling and preserving the seasons. It's a beautiful thing to be able to take advantage of the glut of the season and it's affordable too. What is better than using some tomatoes preserved in August for a pasta in February? I like to do quick pickles and I particularly like carrots and turnips.

WHO WAS A MAJOR INFLUENCE ON YOU, BOTH IN TERMS OF FOOD AND OTHERWISE?

Elizabeth David was a major influence on my cooking and philosophy early on in my cooking career. Maria Montessori has been a major influence, first in my brief teaching career and then quite unexpectedly with the Edible Schoolyard. Now I take inspiration from activists who aren't necessarily involved in food. I'm interested in people who have built major social movements and changed the world for the better.

YOU'VE BEEN AN ADVOCATE FOR LOCAL, SLOW, ORGANIC FOOD FOR A LONG TIME. HOW HAS THE FOOD INDUSTRY CHANGED OVER TIME?

Sadly, it's been hijacked by the fast-food industry and big agriculture—they've tried to make us prisoners to their profits and it's only really happened in the past 50 or so years. But the good news is that all around the world people are waking up and reacting against it strongly. More and more people are concerned about where their food comes from and are willing to pay the local farmers for their work. That makes me incredibly hopeful. We have a long way to go, but I feel optimistic. ○○○

The Art of Simple Food II: Recipes, Flavor and Inspiration from the New Kitchen Garden *(Clarkson Potter) is available now.*

ALMOND MILK PANNA COTTA

RECIPE BY ALICE WATERS

PHOTOGRAPH BY ALICE GAO & FOOD STYLING BY DIANA YEN, THE JEWELS OF NEW YORK

A lice says, "I've been doing this since the early days. It's based off of Richard Olney's blancmange recipe and feels like a family recipe. Making your almond milk is very simple and is what makes this dessert fresh, light and utterly compelling. Add a few slices of peach, nectarine or other stone fruits for a perfect finish, and a spoonful of raspberry or chocolate sauce."

2/3 cup (3.3 ounces/95grams) whole almonds

2 1/3 cups (10.6 ounces/315 milliliters) water

Almond oil or a flavorless vegetable oil

2 tablespoons (30 milliliters) water

One 1/4-ounce (7-gram) packet gelatin

1 3/4 cups (1,415 milliliters) heavy cream

4 1/2 tablespoons (55 grams) sugar

A small pinch of salt

2 to 3 drops of almond extract, if desired

METHOD Measure 2/3 cup whole almonds and 2 1/3 cups water into a bowl. Cover the bowl and soak the almonds overnight. The next day, strain the almonds and save the liquid. Peel off the skins and discard. In a blender, purée the almonds with all the soaking water. Line a strainer with cheesecloth and strain the blended mixture. Once most of the liquid has drained through, gather up the corners of the cheesecloth and squeeze the almond pulp to extract the remaining liquid. Measure 1 3/4 cups of almond milk and set aside.

Lightly brush eight 4-ounce ramekins or custard cups with almond oil or a flavorless vegetable oil. Measure two tablespoons water into a small heat-proof bowl. Sprinkle one 1/4-ounce (7 gram) packet gelatin over the surface of the water to "bloom." If there are any dry spots on the gelatin, sprinkle them with a few drops of water to saturate. Set the bowl aside.

Measure 1 3/4 cups heavy cream, 4 1/2 tablespoons sugar and a small pinch of salt into a heavy-bottomed pot. Heat the mixture over medium heat to 170°F/75°C, stirring to dissolve the sugar and salt. Remove from the heat and let the mixture cool. Once the cream mixture has cooled to 130°F/55°C, gently dissolve the bloomed gelatin by placing your heat-proof bowl into a pan of shallow hot water. Stir gently and when the gelatin is completely liquefied, add it to the warm cream mixture.

Stir in the almond milk and a few drops of almond extract. Strain the mixture and pour into the prepared ramekins or custard cups and put them in the refrigerator to chill until set, about 4 to 5 hours, or overnight. To serve, run a small knife around the inside of each ramekin. Turn each ramekin over onto a small serving plate, shake gently and lift off the ramekin.

Variation: Use the extra almond milk to make a fantastic smoothie with a handful of berries, a few slices of peaches and a couple of dates. ○○○

Serves 8

This is an excerpt from Alice Waters' The Art of Simple Food II (Clarkson Potter).

SHAKE IT UP

A highly imitated design aesthetic, a nonmaterialistic lifestyle, spiritual equality and the invention of the clothespin, pen nib and apple corer: These are just a few reasons to appreciate what the Shakers left behind.

WORDS BY KATIE SEARLE-WILLIAMS & PHOTOGRAPHS BY RYAN BENYI

The cultures that came before us indisputably affect us. They create us, teach us and provide us with the environment we exist in. Even groups that seem distant—separated by space, time or culture—leave a mark on our lives and shape the discourse that, in turn, shapes us.

Shakerism may be an often-mocked religion foreshadowed by epileptic dance styles and oversize bonnets, but few realize the group's all-encompassing influence on daily American life. Founded in England in the 1740s, Shakerism was brought to America in 1774 by Mother Ann Lee, who hoped to share her revelations and spread the gospels in the New World. The religion took some time to gain its footing, but eventually appealed to many during an intense time of religious exploration. It peaked in 1840 with more than 6,000 Shaker members living in 19 communal villages across the Eastern states. Their day-to-day living was rudimentary, free from the so-called distractions of possessions (they embrace communal ownership) and sex (they choose celibacy).

Despite their small numbers, the community's emphasis on simplicity, practicality and highly focused time (due to their lack of "distraction") allowed them to create some of the most functional inventions and designs of the 18th and 19th centuries. Shaker-made furnishings are known for being beautiful, functional, unobtrusive and synonymous with quality: Their designs and furniture were part of a greater architectural movement that emphasized bold, high-grade workmanship and natural materials. They believed that God resided in the details of their work and their craftsmanship, so the precision present in Shaker-made products was unmistakable.

SHAKER INVENTIONS INCLUDED:

Metal pen nibs	*Oval-shaped boxes*	*Circular saws*
Flat brooms	*Mail-order seeds*	*Apple corers*
An early washing machine (called a wash mill)	*Freestanding stairs*	*Waterproof and wrinkle free cloth*
	Clothespins	

Because the Shakers rely on adoption and conversion for maintaining their membership—as they don't believe in procreation—their numbers have dwindled dramatically: Today there are reportedly only four living members. In the past, Shakers sent missionaries from the community to seek out new members and took in orphans, foster kids, families in crisis and indentured children. Although all evidence points toward the community's extinction, the Shakers' lasting influence will be a legacy that has transformed culture for all time.

If you pick and choose life lessons from the Shakers (skip the communes, twirling, arm flapping and no sex thing, if that's not your scene), there's much to learn from their way of doing things. It may seem old-fashioned or out of touch, but the items they used and produced were made to last and many are still in regular use today. They focused on utility and function, perfecting themselves and their work. It may be easy to poke fun, but it also may be worth taking a second look at the Shakers, appreciating their resourceful items as an example of supreme workmanship. They may never pass down human genes, but the world has inherited quite a bit. ○○○

Katie Searle-Williams is one of the founders of Kinfolk. *She lives in Portland, Oregon.*

These photographs were taken at the Shaker Village of Pleasant Hill, Kentucky. Their nonprofit organization aims to preserve the Shakers' legacy through this historical site.

THE LOST ART OF READING ALOUD

WORDS BY CARLY DIAZ & PHOTOGRAPH BY BRITT CHUDLEIGH

Remember those Jane Austen stories where the entertainment revolved around dances, piano recitals and reading aloud? Our writer explains how she learned to experience literature in a fresh new way: as a listener.

The words rang out deep and rich, his voice delivering each syllable with precision and grace. Sentences wrapped around me and the story took shape in the invisible space before my eyes. As the tension of the chapter mounted, his voice paused. The other listeners and I looked at each other, resisting the urge to plead, "*Please, read on.*" We held our breath and sat in silence, our minds racing as the words resumed and carried us toward the finale.

This scene reminded me of my childhood when my older sister and I would curl around our parents and listen as they brought words on a page to life. Over the years, my reading skills grew stronger and the books I borrowed from the library were measured in chapters rather than pages. The length of these stories almost seemed to require reading to turn into a solitary activity. The shift away from reading aloud follows the transition from childhood to adulthood, but it is also a development that can be observed over the centuries: What used to be a form of entertainment in social settings is now primarily an individual pastime.

Nearly a decade ago, while spending a few months at a commune in New England, I rediscovered the pleasure of reading aloud. After the evening meal, the other residents and I would pour a warm drink and settle back into our chairs as someone pulled out a book and began to read. The melody and rhythm of their voice soothed us and drew us into the story.

Outside, the wind howled and the sky dropped snow in amounts I'd never experienced in the mild winters of Oregon. In contrast, the gathering inside was cozy and intimate, made more so by our collective activity. We read a book about a sailor and, while I can't recall the title, I can *see* the story. It comes alive as my memory flickers across the images I conjured as I listened.

As the listeners, we hung on to each word. Drifting off for a moment could mean missing a crucial aspect of the story. But as we let ourselves be fully enveloped by the narration, the process of telling wrapped us up and we experienced the story in a new way.

When I returned home, I shared my rediscovery of the pleasure of reading aloud with my younger sister. Assuming the role of the reader was a new experience altogether. I had to consider aspects that I'd never encountered when reading alone: the pacing of words, sounds for different characters and fluctuations of my voice to convey a sense of drama, suspense or resolution. When I'm the reader, I prefer to select a book I'm already familiar with. Knowing in advance how the story develops focuses my attention on the performative aspect of reading aloud. I'm able to bring a tale to life with family and friends that's meaningful to me, sharing both a story and an experience. ○○○

Carly Diaz is a creative director and content strategist with a love for the written word, visual storytelling and all things digital. She lives in Portland, Oregon.

DIM SUM DIARY

WORDS BY WAI HON CHU & ILLUSTRATIONS BY SARAH BURWASH

*From his early years in Hong Kong to his current life in
Manhattan, chef, instructor and cookbook author Wai Hon Chu
reflects on how the dim sum tradition has been a rare
constant in his family for generations.*

My family left Hong Kong in 1974, the same year that President Nixon and his family waved good-bye to the nation from the steps of the presidential helicopter. That September, having received our immigration papers from the U.S. Justice Department, my parents packed up our cramped one-bedroom apartment, tearfully said good-bye to our relatives and friends and boarded a Boeing 747 bound for New York City. Our future was uncertain, just like the Nixons'.

Many immigrant families who uproot their lives from one country to another will try their best to assimilate, embracing new customs, language, religion and culture. But what seems to have the greatest endurance over time is our devotion to our native cuisine. We tend to find comfort in the food that's most familiar and dear to us.

One meal that's been a constant in my family for generations is dim sum. The phrase literally means "a touch of the heart" because you share a variety of small, meticulously prepared dishes with family and close friends around a communal table. It's a tradition that became popular in teahouses in southern China, where travelers along the Silk Road mingled with local residents when stopping for a cup of tea and some food.

In Hong Kong, every week my mother would shuffle my sister and me to the neighborhood dim sum parlor across the street where we'd start the morning with some strong *pu-erh* tea and dumplings or a plate of steamed rice rolls. "Here's where your grandfather always sat," she'd point out, "right next to the kitchen where he had first pick of the dishes." My mom, like my grandmother, adored the pork and shrimp shao mai dumplings, while my sister devoured the crispy daikon cakes. I could eat an entire dish of stir-fried "silver needle" noodles, but being a finicky eater, I'd pick out the mushrooms before digging into the worm-like noodles.

Life in New York was a bit more hectic. Our home was a small tenement apartment in Chinatown. Dad found work as a butcher and later as a cook at a Chinese restaurant. Mom worked as a seamstress but still found time to take care of the two of us. We'd have dim sum on occasion, but mostly we'd order it for takeout on weekends, bringing the small feast back home to enjoy.

Still, once or twice a year, all of us would go out for dim sum on holidays like Chinese New Year or when family friends came to visit. What was once a weekday ritual had become a meal reserved for special occasions.

Today, as a chef and cooking instructor, I've deciphered many recipes from a lifetime of good eating. Nonetheless, every time I walk into a busy dim sum parlor, I'm immediately enticed by the multitude of dishes piled high atop the steaming pushcarts. As I angle for the table nearest the kitchen, I'm reminded of the meals that my family has enjoyed for generations. When the servers shout out the names of the dishes ("Taro balls!" "Spare ribs!" "Steamed pork buns!"), they are in fact calling my name. ○○○

Wai Hon Chu is the co-author of The Dumpling: A Seasonal Guide *(William Morrow) and teaches cooking classes in New York City.*

See page 136 for Wai's recipe for his mom's favorite, Bottlenecked Pork and Shrimp Dumplings / Shao Mai.

HAR GAU
Shrimp Bonnet

HAAM SUI GOK
Fried Glutinous Rice Dumpling

DAN TAT
Egg Tartlet

CHAR SIU BAO
Steamed Pork Bun

CHEUNG FAN
Steamed Rice Rolls

LOH MAI GAI
Lotus Leaf-wrapped Rice Package
Stuffed with Chicken

SHAO MAI
Bottlenecked Pork and Shrimp Dumpling

THE SWEET SPOT

In life, we often jump into things too early before our plans are ripe. It's the same with fruit: We pick things too quickly because we simply can't wait. Our farm-raised writer explains why sometimes both fruit and friendships need to be found at the perfect moment.

PHOTOGRAPHS BY PARKER FITZGERALD & STYLING BY RILEY MESSINA
WORDS BY ROMY ASH

When I was little, my family lived on a tropical fruit farm. It was a hobby farm really, but our house stood atop a small hill and all around us grew custard apples, mangos, avocados, lemons, limes, oranges and ruby red grapefruits. I loved to watch the purple-red hanging flower of the banana tree reveal its yellow hands. Bulbous papayas grew off tall trunks, the leaves fanning over the fruit like umbrellas. At the very back of the house grew a giant macadamia tree that was resplendent with hanging blossoms in spring and adorned with shiny baubles in winter that revealed a delicious eyeball-size nut when cracked.

"There's a lesson to be learned in the patience it takes to wait for the right moment and there's some courage required in seizing that moment when it comes"

Living on the farm, all the fruit came to the table at exactly the right moment. I learned the art of telling when fruit is ripe. There's a smell, a touch and a right look. A ripe custard apple feels heavy. It's the shape and size of a human heart and colored a rich dark brown. This gothic fruit looks like it must be rotten, but when cut open, its fragrant cream flesh is perfect. An orange can be a trickster—some of the best fruit retains a green hue to the skin. An avocado must give a little when pressed gently at the spot where the stem meets the fruit, and when ready the skin will be dull and become a darker green. A ripe mango will perfume a whole room. A papaya should smell fragrant when ripe too and, like an avocado, it should give a little at the point of the stem. Pears vary according to variety, but the Packham (similar to the Yellow Bartlett in the US) should be yellow and blush when ripe. If you're buying from a shop or a market, only buy fruit that smells mouthwatering. Hold the fruit, take in its scent and if your grocer gives you a look, it's time to change purveyors.

Just like in the market, it's right to feel these things out in life too. There's a lesson to be learned in the patience it takes to wait for the right moment and there's some courage required in seizing that moment when it comes. Snap a banana open before it's time and the resulting furred mouth is the punishment for being impulsive. In life we often jump into things early before our plans are ripe. We declare our undying love for a new friend when we should be taking things gently. Or we leave old friendships unattended, forgetting about them, letting them go soft. But there's often a second chance for both friendships and fruit: Aging pears can always be caramelized with sugar on the stove-top, blackening bananas can be made into banana bread and a friend lured back with the resulting alchemy.

Opportunity must be taken, and sometimes that opportunity doesn't look the way we expect. Sometimes it looks like a dark custard apple heart on the outside, and we must learn to trust ourselves and trust our instincts, because to wait for the right moment has a sweet reward. ○○○

When Romy Ash is not writing about food, she writes fiction. Her debut novel, Floundering, *was published in 2012. She lives in Melbourne, Australia.*

HOW TO BE NEIGHBORLY: MIND YOUR ELDERS

WORDS BY JULIE POINTER & PHOTOGRAPH BY JULIE MARIE CRAIG

There are times when the older folks in your life need some looking after.
Here are some ideas for ways to make their day, whether it's with gifts,
shoveling their path or just plain old listening.

We all have that elusive neighbor who sometimes appears across the hedge, usually bathrobe-clad while calling for the kitty. There's something distinguished about the way those white tufts crown his head just so, and you often wonder where he acquired such an extensive collection of Norwegian sweaters. It would be easy to eternally remain a mere observer, simply speculating on the curious details of his life from afar. But truth be told, each fresh generation is indebted to those who have gone before, and the younger folk would be wise to take an interest in the collective history of the past. Even better, learn at the feet of those who have been there. And besides, perhaps it's his grandchildren supplying all of those woolly knits in exchange for the fact they can't visit in person.

There couldn't be a better time than the cozy winter season to bridge the divide, step beyond your comfort and share a bit of cheer with your neighbor who may be in the winter of their life.

– During the holidays, everyone likes a bit of festive cheer to adorn the house. When you're out collecting pine branches, a tree, holly or what-have-you for your own abode, make sure to gather a bit extra. Fashion a simple wreath or a birch-log candleholder and bring it over to Mabel or Laurence along with a plate of warm ginger snaps. Or it doesn't matter if you're not well versed in the kitchen—be a patron of your local bakery and pick up something nice for two instead.

– Our frenzied forms of current communication have nearly done away with the need for patience in conversation and correspondence, but our older and wiser predecessors are more practiced in the art of listening. Give your aged neighbor the gift of your ears: Ask for a story with the willingness to pay full attention, no matter how tangential the tale may become.

– The winter can be a hard time to maintain things around the yard, particularly in snowy climes. Offer a hand to shovel the drive, salt the roadway or clean out the gutters before the weather gets nasty. If you're so inclined toward twinkle lights, offer to hang some in the barren cherry tree or around the front door. Sometimes the smallest gestures mean the most.

– There's always an abundance of warm foods on the stove during the colder months and a pot of soup is just asking to be made large enough to share. Brave the cold and bring a cauldron of chowder and a hearty chunk of bread to your neighbor. Deliver it in your favorite Le Creuset so you have an excuse to come back soon.

– Make a concerted effort to find out something unexpected about your neighbor: Does she have an enviable fascination with wind-up watches, the Black Sea or whip-poor-wills? Scour your local used bookstore or a favorite corner shop and find a little something thoughtful that communicates your interest in their life. An attentive act goes far. ○○○

Julie Pointer is the Community Director at Kinfolk. *She is a maker, writer, sometimes stylist and ceaseless hostess living in Portland, Oregon.*

YEAR IN, YEAR OUT

PHOTOGRAPH BY RYAN BENYI

Every family has its ritual quirks and the holiday season normally brings the odder ones out. We ask some of our friends around the world how they say good-bye to one year and welcome another.

MARÍA DEL MAR SACASA – NICARAGUAN I've been handed down a bunch of cookbooks—I have piles and piles—but this is the oldest one *(pictured)*. My great-great-grandmother handwrote it in the 1920s. The family has always stayed together through cooking together and eating together, so cookbooks have been an interesting way to see how our tradition has carried on through the kitchen. This particular old cookbook contains a recipe for *Pudín de su Majestad (Majesty's Cake)*. It's her take on a traditional dessert that's meant to be served during the holidays called *Pío Quinto*, which is a custard cake named after Pope Pius V of the 1500s, but I don't think anyone knows why! My great-great-grandmother's version uses crystallized fruits instead of the traditional rum (our national spirit) and raisins. Nicaragua is a heavily Catholic country and our beliefs and culture stem from that religious tradition. The entire Christmas season relates to the Virgin Mary and is colorful, joyous and exploding with centuries of family traditions.

JOANNA HAN – KOREAN My fondest wintertime memories revolve around New Year's Day—specifically the Korean New Year, or *Seollal*. The morning always began with *jullae*, the tradition of the youngest family members bowing to their elders and wishing them happiness in the year to come. The first bows went to the oldest family members, then the next oldest and so on, ending with parents, aunts and uncles. The children received money and were advised to spend it wisely (mine invariably disappeared after a single trip to the bookstore). After jullae, we feasted on a breakfast of hot *ddukgook* (dumpling soup), then endless rounds of an age-old traditional board game called *yutnori* always followed. New Year's Day is still my favorite winter holiday thanks to these memories—I can't think of anything lovelier than spending the first day of the year with excellent food and my favorite people.

NABIL SABIO AZADI – IRANIAN Although I was born and raised in New Zealand, my Iranian parents deftly managed to keep us children hooked on one particular Iranian tradition—*Nowrūz*. It's the New Year in the Persian calendar, celebrated on the Spring Equinox in Iran and effectively the only time when the young categorically must receive some sort of present from their elders. It was our Christmas, and we loved it! It also involves a bizarre table setting tradition: *Haft Sîn* means "the seven Ss" and involves setting the table with seven items starting with the letter S in the Persian alphabet. Typically, this will involve *sabzeh* (wheat, barley or lentils growing in a dish), *samanu* (a type of pudding), *sîb* (apples), *sîr* (garlic), *sekkeh* (coins), *serkeh* (vinegar) and *somaq* (sumac). This was a personal highlight, second only to the *kookoo sabzi* that my mother would make. It's a kind of soufflé made out of vegetables and leafy greens as well as dill, spinach, spring onions, nuts and coriander.

HEESCO KHOSNARAN - MONGOLIAN Mongolia follows a combination of lunar and solar calendars, meaning our New Year starts on a different day every year, but always in the middle of winter when it's as cold as -40ºF. The celebration is called *Tsagaan Sar*, which means "white moon," and for three days you visit relatives and eat nonstop. My favorite part was *Bituun*, our New Year's Eve. You're meant to eat till you're completely full, as you're not allowed to greet the New Year with an empty stomach! It was also the day our family would make hundreds of *buuz* (dumplings) and everyone would come to pay their respect to the elders. The older you are the more visitors you'd get. And more visitors mean more dumplings! We would make one "lucky" dumpling with a metal coin in it and whoever got it would have the best year. I learned to cheat by pre-poking the cooked dumplings with a fork! I live in Australia now, but when my daughter grows up a bit, I'll teach her to make buuz our way.

JULIE POINTER - AMERICAN My mother's father has been making maple syrup every winter for my entire life (and pancakes year-round to enjoy it with!). The vision of him sitting in the side yard surrounded by snow, maple trees, squirrels and the occasional deer is seared in my mind as a very special tradition I now see carried on in my adult life. I seem to consistently be making or building something myself, and holidays are my opportunity to bake old family favorites. The love of real maple syrup has also been deeply ingrained in me because I seem to use it to sweeten everything.

JANE DU TOIT - BOTSWANAN Since Christmas in Botswana is a hot one, we do things a bit differently—though without fail my grandmother Anne would make a turkey for lunch, even if it was in 48ºC heat (118ºF)! Our family is made up of curious backpackers that came to Maun, Botswana, and never left, meaning our traditions are a weird but perfect mix of cultures, food and people. We'd mix European items such as *panettone* with traditional African foods such as *braais, magwinya* and *biltong*. It was more about family than food. Anne also has a yearly Christmas party for all the Maun children, buying each child a present and a designated Santa would deliver them in a weird way. One year, Santa came riding a donkey (a bit drunkenly from the adults' Christmas party), the next in a boat up the river and one year even in a helicopter! It was a great time to be a kid in Africa.

MADELEINE RYAN - JEWISH I have vivid memories of celebrating Rosh Hashanah and Passover with my mum's side of the family. We had gefilte fish with optional horseradish at every celebration, plus apples and honey to represent the New Year during Rosh Hashanah. At Passover we would eat matzos (unleavened bread) and I'd be sent out to search for the one special piece, called the afikomen. As I'm an only child I was blessed with always being the youngest and therefore always the number one candidate to search for the matzo piece, find it, and receive a money-filled envelope. My love of envelopes began then and ended when I started receiving bills later on in life.

LORENZO MASNAH – COLOMBIAN The *novenas* are the nine days before Christmas when the whole family gathers in a different house every night in Colombia. It's one big party! We drink a lot of *Aguardiente* and rum, staying up till the morning dancing cumbias and salsas. My grandma makes *buñuelos*: They're kind of like a spongy, salty donut that gets baked or fried. Another weird activity happens on New Year's: *Año Viejo*. We make a doll out of old clothes that looks like an old man and fill it with rice… and fireworks! In the countryside, every family makes one and sits it by the road for the last days of the year, and at midnight on the 31st, it's lit on fire. It's a pretty cool show.

JULIET COOMBE – SRI LANKAN At the New Year I always think of the eye-catching chains of limes and red or green chilies that help ward off bad spirits. In Sri Lanka, food is used for casting spells: Curry and rice are used to entice the bad spirits out of your body and limes can be found stuck on tridents outside *kovils* (Hindu temples). Cinnamon also makes me think of Christmas, like beets or fish straight out of the sea baked on cinnamon logs on Christmas day. The family comes together from all over the island to have milk rice at dawn and during the day we play games and fly kites. The elders are very sociable and tell stories about this being "Adam's land," the original Garden of Eden!

LOUISA THOMSEN BRITS – DANISH We always celebrated Christmas on Christmas Eve with the tree at the heart of our gathering. Early in the evening we'd carry the tree inside to decorate it with straw snowflakes, red hearts, paper stars and real candles. After dinner, the candles were lit and then we all danced around and around it, faster and faster into the night until it was time to open gifts. Our mother made *risalamande* (a Danish adaption of the French *riz a l'amande*), which is a cold rice pudding rich with whipped cream, almonds and vanilla and served with warm cherry sauce. Somewhere in the big bowl, a single whole almond was hidden. We ate carefully hoping to be the one to find it and win a prize—a chocolate heart, a marzipan pig or a small board game.

SAMUEL KRIFTOSKI – MACEDONIAN Family celebrations were always loud with singing, dancing and a lot of noisy, messy eating. Anyone Macedonian, Croatian or Serbian in the community was invited and considered family, no matter what tension was going on. Stuffed peppers, potato twisties, sugared peanuts, apple strudel… The food was very good, but sometimes the wine wasn't so good (especially if it was the sugary home brew made by my grandfather). After we had all eaten, we'd always go for a long walk around my grandfather's farm in New Zealand, meandering along the citrus groves picking fruit as we went. We would all gather back in the house to watch him cut up a freshly picked watermelon and somehow manage to find room in our bellies to eat it, with sticky hands and juice dripping down our chins. ○○○

HOT TODDY HISTORY

WORDS BY DANIEL SEARING & PHOTOGRAPH BY JULIE MARIE CRAIG

A classic drink for old-timers, the Hot Toddy can contain all kinds of ingredients. Our spirits expert gives us a rundown on the history of these winter warmers and some recipes to go with it. Chin-chin!

Like its cousin the Mint Julep and its descendant the Old Fashioned, the Hot Toddy is a simple drink made complicated by the seemingly endless variations it has engendered. It often seems as if there are as many recipes as there are toddy makers and, like holiday sweets, most of us prefer the version we've been served most often. I'm not going to admonish you to abandon your Nana's cure for the common cold but I will insist you enjoy it in a bit more educated fashion.

According to noted cocktail historian David Wondrich's entertaining history, *Imbibe*, the toddy as it was consumed more than two centuries ago was little more than spirit, sugar and water (the latter not even always hot) and unadorned with citrus, though occasionally freshly grated nutmeg was deployed. I confess I prefer mine with a twist of lemon peel, though this was known as a Skin, usually preceded by its spirit base, as in "Whisky Skin."

That leads us to the question of that base spirit. Frequently enjoyed with brandy or rum in its heyday, the Hot Toddy is thought to have originated in Scotland, which certainly boasts the weather and the whisky for it. While many spirits will work, Wondrich recommends (and I concur) a spirit made in a pot still, which happens to be the type they use for single malt Scotch. Lucky for we spirits enthusiasts, it's also the type favored by the new wave of American craft distillers who are bringing a renaissance to spirits-making akin to the craft beer boom of the past couple of decades.

The other important characteristic is age. While you don't have to reach for the oldest bottle on your bar, there's something about the flavor of barrel-aged spirits that lends itself to the Hot Toddy. Some of it's the wood, of course, and the flavors of spice, vanilla and caramel that come from a charred or toasted barrel that are so pleasant in a warm drink. But it's also time: time for a spirit to settle down and shed some of the wild, youthful flavors that can be unpleasant and aggressive when wafted to your nose on a pipe of steam. Heat and dilution will intensify the aroma of a spirit. However, the best toddies aren't made with the cheap stuff and, like a good steak or a farm-fresh vegetable, fine spirits are best appreciated simply.

"So what if I like tea or citrus juice in my toddy?" you ask. Just as we once came to accept that anything served in a stemmed, V-shaped glass could be called a martini, most everyone understands a Hot Toddy to be a warming, restorative drink with spirits, sweetener and some other stuff in there. But if that other stuff is tea, ginger ale, lemon juice or similar (which will also do the trick), you'd be more accurate calling it a Hot Punch. This doesn't mean you can't have a lot of fun with varied ingredients. Even if you are a dyed-in-the-wool loyalist to your favorite spirit, it's surprising how much difference the sweetener can make in a classic Hot Toddy. After all, it's a third of the ingredients and one of the others is water. Try alternatives to white sugar such as demerara and turbinado, or substitute non-sugar syrups such as agave nectar and maple. And then there's honey, which—via farmers markets and farm-to-table ingredient awareness—offers an ever-widening world of variety unto itself. ○○○

Daniel Searing is the author of The Punch Bowl: 75 Recipes Spanning Four Centuries of Wanton Revelry *(Sterling Epicure) and owner of Room 11 in Washington, D.C.*

Turn to page 137 to see Daniel's recipes for a Hot Toddy, Hot Rum Punch and a Pomegranate Toddy.

ACQUIRED TASTES: ONLY TIME WILL TELL

WORDS BY DAVID COGGINS & PHOTOGRAPH BY PARKER FITZGERALD

Pretending to like things you hate to make you feel like an adult?
Sometimes it's better to consider things a second or third time.

Recently I sat at the bar of a smart new Danish restaurant in New York. It was an attractive place with clean Scandinavian design, appealing staff and the requisite jars of homemade Aquavit lining the wall. Proud of its heritage, it served traditional food for Manhattan diners who in all likelihood were not familiar with dishes such as Rullepølse and Æblekage.

Prominently featured on the menu was a herring platter, the strongly flavored staple fish of the nation. When in Denmark, or at least our version of it here in Manhattan, I figured I should do as the Danes do, and took the herring plunge. It was perfectly good, but it wasn't until I finished that I thought of asking myself: Do I even like herring? Yes, I suppose I do, but never quite as much as I wish I did. It's as if that by continuing to order it, I believe I'll learn to like it and finally attain a level of dining enlightenment.

Essentially, I had fallen into an acquired taste holding pattern, neither loving nor rejecting the potential object of desire. Who was to blame: the fish or my own lack of gastronomic worldliness? I certainly *wanted* to give my heart to herring, but something was standing in the way.

Acquired tastes are a curious consideration, from dining to music, clothing to film. Some foods, such as coffee, mushrooms, squid or whiskey, which are generally at odds with youthful taste buds, become appreciated over time. In these cases familiarity doesn't breed contempt—over time it evolves and brings pleasure.

Other tastes don't evolve—suddenly they just hit you at once and make perfect sense. It's like when you're 15 years old and every Smiths song sounds exactly right. Other appreciations only apply for a certain place and a certain time, like when I began reading Anthony Powell's series of 12 novels, *A Dance to the Music of Time*. Powell's books are not for everybody. In fact, they veer dangerously close to being boring. But I was in my late twenties, living in London, and the sensibility suited me perfectly. It's like nattō, the fermented Japanese soybeans that have an absolutely vile smell. I can't stand nattō myself, despite many Japanese friends assuring me how wonderful it is. But as with Powell's novels, if certain things hit you right, good lord, they're incredible. That's the interesting thing about acquired tastes. It's not just that sometimes you develop them and sometimes you don't. It's that sometimes you desperately want to like something and finally have to admit that, no, in fact, kale is not for you. There, you've said it, and relieving the burden can be very sweet.

But your mind remains open to giving yourself a second chance to form a first impression. That's why you fear not when offered orange wine, shad roe or duck hearts—you know it may be the beginning of a beautiful friendship. ○○○

YOUR MOTHER'S MOTHER

WORDS BY GEORGIA FRANCES KING & PHOTOGRAPHS BY SHANTANU STARICK

*A supper club in Berlin serves up dishes straight from grandmothers'
memories. We speak with Mother's Mother founder Kavita Meelu
about keeping it in the family but sharing it with others.*

Whether you think your mother's mother's food was astronomical or bland, you can't call it unmemorable. It represents a time in our young, impressionable minds when cultural identities are solidifying along with our taste buds. "Often enough, your grandmother's food isn't the best you've had, but there's an element of romance about it that has connotations of heritage and identity," says Kavita Meelu, the founder of Mother's Mother, a Berlin-based supper club that focuses on the memories and meals of grandmothers past. Every few weeks she invites an international chef to create a menu inspired by their childhood table, reconnecting with their upbringing and introducing those traditions to a slew of culture-hungry diners. "Plus, it's a great way to pay respect to your mothers and grandmothers," she says.

Growing up in Birmingham, England, as a second-generation Punjabi immigrant, Kavita feels connected to the grandmother she never met through the recipes she taught to Kavita's mother, like unripe mangoes stewed in spices and yogurt smoked in burned ghee. "Food is a very strong part of my identity, and it's also the link to a family I never really got to know," she says. After living in London for nearly a decade, she moved to Berlin four years ago only to discover their culinary output didn't reflect their creative expression. Luckily, she had an idea to fix that.

The tasty seed for Mother's Mother had been planted nearly a decade earlier over dim sum with her circle of friends from Nigeria, Colombia, Ghana and beyond. "We had this sense of food pride. The defense of your culture can come through convincing people that food from your country is the best food out there," she says, laughing. "For me, that's one of the easiest way to consume or understand another culture: Eat it!" Over dinner, they would often fantasize about the fictitious restaurant they'd open, solely serving dishes their respective multinational grandmothers once cooked. And now Kavita had the chance to make that a reality.

So far there have been nearly 20 Mother's Mother supper club nights honoring grannies everywhere from Naples (*mulignane c'a' ciucculata*—chocolate layered with fried eggplant and candied fruits) to Indonesia (*babi guling* and *jukut nangka mekuah*—milk suckling pig with Balinese spices and jackfruit coconut milk). Each dinner serves around 30 people every few weeks with attendees chosen through a lottery system due to the high demand for a seat.

The event pictured was a Ghanaian feast by David Okine. Growing up in Africa, his mom ran a street food store famous for delicacies from her native Togo. He'd always help his mother make one of these—*kenkey,* fermented maize balls wrapped in corn leaves and steamed—since his father was absent for most of his childhood. Kenkey may not sound like the most appetizing dish, but when served with a backstory and some love (and a whole fish braised with spicy *peppe* sauce), it's as if you're eating a memory instead of just a food. "If you know a little bit behind why people are serving you a meal, it makes it taste better," Kavita says. "It's not just the food—it's all of these things that come to the plate with you." ○○○

To find out more or to attend an event, head to mothersmother.com.

POST NOTES

PHOTOGRAPH BY LUISA BRIMBLE

Emily Post was a titan of 20th-century etiquette. We ask her great-great-granddaughter Lizzie Post for some modern entertaining tips that aren't as stern and stodgy as those of yesteryear.

KNOW YOUR ENTERTAINING FROM YOUR GET-TOGETHERS It's hard for us to do dinner parties now and really *do* them. We feel silly with the formality that used to be put on. Entertaining in general is so much more casual than what it used to be. It should be about taking care of someone else and choosing to dote on them for a night, whereas a get-together is more casual.

RECIPROCATE FOR YOUR MATES I wish we could bring back the reciprocal side of hosting. You look at how it's mimicked on *Mad Men*, and that's the world I remember hearing about from my grandmother. If my grandmother threw a party, someone else would throw a cocktail party to reciprocate. It was that kind of world.

IF IT'S YOUR HOUSE, THEN YOU'RE THE HOST The modern definition of hosting would be providing the space. A lot of the time when we go to friends' houses, we eat on laps. I mean, not all the time, but sometimes that's what it is. But if Emily Post wanted to *entertain* someone as a host, it should be at the table. Not pomp and circumstance, but it should be planned. Someone should feel like they're being taken care of.

ADD A DASH OF SPICE TO YOUR POTLUCK Sometimes I love it when someone hosts a dinner and really *hosts* it. I'd hate to see our generation lose what it means to host. Now that I'm 30, I have some friends who are just dead set on potluck dinners. It's always a community and everyone brings everything and that's great. But it's funny, because every now and again I go to someone's house and they don't ask you to bring anything and they've done everything themselves, and I'm like, "Wow! That was really nice! This is what entertaining means!"

PIZZA SHOULDN'T BE EATEN WITH A KNIFE AND FORK "Eat the food the way it's meant to be eaten"—that's what my great-great-grandmother would always say. So if pizza is a finger food then she's going to say, "Okay! Pizza on laps, paper plates, picnic style." And that's totally fine.

DON'T BE LATE Emily's other big thing was food being served on time, so much so that if the maids were early with her lunch, they would wait on the stairs until the clock struck one and then they'd walk in. That's the only thing I've ever heard her be strict about.

KEEP THE PRINCIPLE, LOSE THE RIGOR It's important to continue the essence of traditions. I'm really nostalgic and can hold on way too closely to the specifics of how something is done. It's important to be able to let go of the specifics, but hold on to the intention. So, does the order that we do things on Christmas morning really matter, or does it matter that we're together and opening presents and having fun? That's something I need to get better at! ○ ○ ○

The 18th edition of Emily Post's Etiquette: Manners for a New World *is available now.*

BOTTLENECKED PORK AND SHRIMP DUMPLINGS
(SHAO MAI)

RECIPE BY WAI HON CHU & CONNIE LOVATT

4 dried shiitake or black mushrooms, soaked in hot water to cover for 30 minutes

1/2 pound (225 grams) coarsely ground pork

1/2 pound (225 grams) fresh shrimp, peeled, deveined and very finely chopped

5 to 6 fresh water chestnuts, peeled and chopped fine, or canned water chestnuts, drained and chopped fine

2 tablespoons (14 grams) cornstarch

1 teaspoon (5 grams) sugar

1 teaspoon (6 grams) salt

1/4 teaspoon freshly ground white pepper

1 tablespoon (15 milliliters) rice wine

2 teaspoons (10 milliliters) soy sauce

1 teaspoon (5 milliliters) toasted sesame oil, plus more for greasing the steamer basket

One (16-ounce/45-gram) package round wonton wrappers (Cantonese-style)

8- to 10-quart (7.5- to 9.5-liter) steamer pot

METHOD Drain the mushrooms and squeeze out any excess liquid. Remove and discard the stems and finely chop the mushroom caps. Place the mushrooms in a medium bowl along with the remaining ingredients except for the wonton wrappers. Mix vigorously with a wooden spoon until the filling is a velvety texture, about 3 minutes. Cover and refrigerate for at least 30 minutes.

Lay flat 1 to 5 dumpling wrappers. Brush each round with a very thin coating of water to make it sticky enough to seal. Place a rounded teaspoon of filling in the center of each round. Gather up the sides of the round, creating a pouch around the filling and leaving an open neck in the center of the gathered dough. Pinch together the creases and pleats that formed naturally while the dough was gathered up, without closing the neck. This gives the dumpling a loose and frilly top. Gently squeeze the body of the dumpling until the filling pushes up through the neck a little. Holding the dumpling by the neck, tap its base on your work surface until it is flat enough on the bottom to sit upright. Place on a towel-lined tray and repeat with the remaining rounds and filling. Keep the dumplings covered with a kitchen towel as you work. Once you have assembled the first batch of dumplings, continue with the remaining wrappers and filling.

Remove the basket from the steamer pot, add 2 inches of water to the pot and bring to a boil over high heat. Lightly grease the basket with sesame oil and arrange as many dumplings in the basket as you can fit without them touching. Place the basket in the pot, cover, reduce the heat to medium-high and steam for 20 minutes.

Remove the pot from the heat. Carefully remove the basket and place it on a folded kitchen towel. Remove the shao mai with a spoon or a small spatula and place them on a serving plate. Serve immediately while you cook the remaining shao mai. ○○○

Serves 4 to 8 (makes about 48 dumplings)

Adapted from The Dumpling: A Seasonal Guide *(William Morrow).*

HOT TODDIES

RECIPES BY DANIEL SEARING

HOT TODDY

1 1/2 ounces (45 milliliters) whiskey, preferably pot distilled such as single malt Scotch or many American craft whiskies like Dancing Pines Bourbon or Oola "Waitsburg" Bourbon

1 teaspoon (5 grams) sugar

3 ounces (90 milliliters) boiling water plus enough to warm the vessel

METHOD Fill a cup, mug or sturdy glass with boiling water to warm, then discard. Add whiskey, sugar and water as above or to taste and stir until sugar is dissolved. If desired, twist a lemon peel and drop it in, or grate some fresh nutmeg into the toddy. *Note:* Use a vegetable peeler from top to bottom to get a half to three-quarter-inch peel as free from white pith as possible. A Microplane makes a great nutmeg grater.

HOT RUM PUNCH

1 ounce (30 milliliters) aromatic gold rum such as Agricole, Jamaican or American craft (like Dancing Pines Cask)

1/2 ounce (15 milliliters) fine brandy such as cognac or American craft (Osocalis is a good choice)

3 ounces (90 milliliters) boiling water plus enough to warm the vessel

1/2 ounce (15 milliliters) lemon juice

1 tablespoon (15 grams) brown sugar or to taste

3 cloves

METHOD Fill a cup, mug or sturdy glass with boiling water to warm, then discard. Add spirits, lemon juice, brown sugar and cloves. Add water and stir until sugar is dissolved. Garnish with a lemon peel. *Note:* Adapted from *To Have and Have Another, A Hemingway Cocktail Companion* by Phil Greene, who adapted it from a recipe published by Hemingway's friend Charles Baker, a celebrated author and bon vivant in his own right. If you must have juice in your hot drink, go with a classic.

POMEGRANATE TODDY

1 ounce (30 milliliters) Jack Rudy Small Batch (or other craft) Grenadine

3 ounces (90 milliliters) boiling water plus enough to warm the vessel

Small piece of crystallized ginger

Orange peel

Cinnamon stick

METHOD Fill a cup, mug or sturdy glass with boiling water to warm, then discard. Add ginger and orange peel and crush the ginger with a muddler or spoon. Add grenadine and boiling water, stir and garnish with the cinnamon stick. *Note*: This non-alcoholic toddy based on a classic cocktail ingredient resurrected from the tomb of Shirely Temples is more fun than another cup of herbal tea for your non-imbibing guests. ○ ○ ○

RECIPE: MAC & CHILI & CHEESE BY MOLLIE KATZEN

Continued from page 99

Place a medium-large saucepan over medium heat and wait about a minute, then add the olive oil and swirl to coat the pan. Toss in the onion and cook, stirring often, for about 3 minutes, or until it begins to soften. Stir in the bell pepper, chili and garlic, along with the spices and 1/2 teaspoon salt. Cook over medium heat, stirring often, for 5 minutes.

Turn the heat to low, then sprinkle in the flour with one hand as you continue to whisk with the other. (Vegetable pieces might get caught up in the tines; just shake them free.) It will quickly become a paste, after which, continue to whisk and cook for another 15 seconds or so.

Keep the pot over low heat as you drizzle in the hot milk with one hand and whisk with the other. Add the remaining 1/2 teaspoon salt, and keep cooking and stirring (use a wooden spoon at this point) for about two minutes, until the mixture is thick and smooth. Sprinkle in half the cheddar and 1/4 cup of the Parmesan, stirring until the cheese is fully incorporated.

Remove the sauce from the heat, then add the cooked pasta, along with the beans and the remaining cheddar. Stir until all the pasta and beans are well coated, being careful to avoid breaking the beans. Sprinkle in some black pepper plus touches of cayenne or crushed red pepper to taste as you go.

Transfer to the prepared baking pan, top with tomato slices and sprinkle on the remaining Parmesan.

Bake uncovered for 15 to 20 minutes, or until bubbly around the edges and crisp and golden on top. Serve hot. ○○○

Serves 6

SPECIAL THANKS
Paintings Katie Stratton

Partnership with Kodak

Kodak
PROFESSIONAL Products

Thanks to West Elm for their support

west elm

ON THE COVER
Photograph by Neil Bedford
Model Helen Storey
Petticoat by AB, available at Egg

AROUND THE BLOCK
Stylist Beverly James Neel

RETIREMENT PASTIMES
Stylist Beverly James Neel

THE SOFT-SERVE MENU
Retoucher Ashlee Gray Retouch

THE GRACE OF GRAY
Stylist Rose Forde
Production Upstairs Production
Photographer's first assistant Chris Rhodes
Photographer's second assistant Chris Nutt
Photographer's retoucher Oliver Carver
Assistant stylist Lauryn Tomlinson
Hair Marcia Lee with Caren
Makeup Gina Blondell

Models, in order of appearance:
Pam Lucas, *Environmental activist and anti-fracking campaigner*
Helen Storey
Sandrae Lawrence, *Cofounder of the Cocktail Lovers*
Thelma Speirs, *Cofounder of Bernstock Speirs*
Sally Green, *Art director*
Anissa Helou, *Food writer and consultant*
Jenni Rhodes, *Model, actress & designer*

Clothing
1 Shirt and dress by Margaret Howell
2 Petticoat by AB, available at Egg
3 Dress by Casey Casey, available at Egg
4 Shirt by Filipa K with coat by Peter Jensen
5 T-shirt by Won Hundred with shirt/dress by Palmer//Harding
6 Dress by Arts and Science, available at Egg
7 Blouse by Arts and Science, available at Egg
Stockist Egg (011 44 207 235 9315)

THE DAYS OF OUR LIVES
Special thanks to Saer Richards (for interviewing Myrtle and Athena); Louisa Thomsen Brits (for interviewing Irma, Lisbet and Inge); Patrick Gookin (for interviewing Robert); Olivia Rae James (for interviewing Nancy); and Jodi L. Murphy (for interviewing Larry)

OLD MADE NEW: LAMB SHEPHERD'S PIE
Prop stylist Kate S. Jordan
Assistant food stylist Brenna Paulsen

FOR YOU, WITH LOVE
Stylist Beverly James Neel

CAKES FOR THE AGES
Sugar decor Sarah Donato (Signe Sugar)

TOP CHEFS: RECIPES BY YOTAM OTTOLENGHI, MOLLIE KATZEN & ALICE WATERS
Prop stylist Kate S. Jordan
Assistant food stylist Brenna Paulsen

THE SWEET SPOT
Thanks to the Kiyokawa Family Orchards for the pears

KEEP IN TOUCH